BLYTHE HAMER

DOGS *at* WAR

TRUE STORIES OF CANINE COURAGE UNDER FIRE

CARLTON
BOOKS

To Brad, Haley, Russell and Christopher

Published in 2001 by Carlton Books Ltd
20 Mortimer Street
London
W1T 3JW

Copyright © Carlton Publishing Group

A CIP catalogue record for this book is available from
the British Library.

ISBN 1 84222 262 7

Printed in Great Britain by Mackays of Chatham

CONTENTS

Chapter One

Early Warriors

FROM THE BEGINNING

For about 15,000 years now, dogs have been living with humans, sharing their shelter and their food. However, ancient dogs were not allowed the leisure that today's pets enjoy – they were expected to contribute toward their room and board. The Egyptians used dogs for war as early as 4000 BC, according to ancient wall art. In Homer's *Odyssey,* written in the eighth century AD, dogs appear as hunters capable of confronting the most ferocious animals, such as lions and bears. Dogs were also guards for important public buildings and herds of sheep.

Giving the dogs jobs gave them the opportunity to prove their tenacity and courage. For this, very early in their working history, dogs were celebrated as heroes. Their memory, intelligence, and loyalty could surpass the skills of the average human being. Dogs often showed complete attachment to their masters — an attachment that took precedence over all other considerations, including the dogs' own safety.

No wonder dogs have often been given crucial military roles. They are well suited to sentry duty, with acute senses of hearing and smell, but they are also good fighters. Ancient dogs were trained to attack their masters' enemies. Before the introduction of gunpowder, dogs could engage in combat side-by-side with their masters without undue disadvantage. The Greeks, Babylonians, and Assyrians used them as attackers, and many of their dogs wore armor complete with spikes.

Caesar described the bravery and courage of English mastiffs when he invaded Britain in 55 BC. Sometimes these armored mastiffs were equipped with mounted knives or flaming torches, which drove the Roman horses wild.

As warfare has evolved, so have the roles that dogs play. North American Indians used dogs as sentries, as well as carriers of their belongings. Russian soldiers used ambulance dogs in the Russo-Japanese war of 1904-5. In the Spanish-Moroccan War (1919–26), dogs were trained to run along the front lines to draw enemy fire, and thus reveal the gun positions of the opposing force. Less heralded, but perhaps most appreciated, is the dog's role as mascot.

This role, as man's best friend and most steadfast companion, has not changed over time. Throughout the course of history, there are countless stories of dogs' loyalty and devotion, bravery and courage. It is these traits that make dogs treasured colleagues, as well as best friends, during wartime.

A MASTIFF

WHY DOGS MAKE GOOD SOLDIERS

For their loyalty, courage, and devotion alone, dogs have long been pre-ferred companions during wartime. But, as history attests, over the cen-turies dogs' roles in war have evolved from simple mascot to sophisti-cated scout. This is not because dogs have changed – it is because man's understanding of the capabilities of dogs has expanded. With each war experience, soldiers have learned more about what dogs can actually do, and how to best motivate and train them.

Aside from his devotion to his master, a dog's best qualifications for military service are his nose and ears. All dogs have a better sense of smell than any human; they probably remember smells better than they remember things they have seen. The sense of smell is called olfaction, and consists of the ability to detect chemicals floating in the air. A dog can smell well because of his relatively long nose, which contains rolls of paper-thin bone over which the chemical molecules float. These fine bones are connected to a mesh of nerve endings which are attached to the olfactory nerve, which is connected to the brain. For dogs, the olfactory center consists of about two billion olfactory receptors, compared to a human being's 40 million receptors. This means that an average dog can smell from 50 to 100 times better than an average person, depending on the breed of dog.

Over the centuries, the way dogs have been bred has depended on what they were going to be used for. For example, scent hounds used for hunting, such as the beagle, pointer, and English setter, need to have an excellent sense of smell to be good at their work. These hounds developed better noses than some other breeds as a result of artificial selection. People determined to raise the best hunting hounds choose puppies with particularly good noses as future breeders. Thus, succeeding generations of these particular breeds developed better senses of smell than would have occurred naturally.

Some dogs appear to rely more heavily on ground scent, while others are sensitive to airborne scent. Breeds used to track the enemy, such as

Cuban bloodhounds in the Second Seminole War, and, later, the Labrador retrievers in the Vietnam war, favor ground scent.

Another important asset is a dog's ability to distinguish one individual scent and follow it despite thousands of competing smells. During World War II, some people thought that dogs could distinguish someone according to his race; it was subsequently discovered that the primary reason behind different racial smells is that people smell differently depending on the type of food they eat.

Dogs of the same breed often have very different olfactory abilities, with some dogs better at scenting people and others better at detecting booby traps or trip wires. The best war dogs used all of their senses simultaneously. Von, a scout dog who worked in Vietnam, could alert at over 500 yards to trip wires, because he combined his sharp sense of smell with the fact that he could hear the air moving over the wires.

Another reason dogs make good soldiers is because they can hear so well. They have a broad hearing spectrum which allows them to hear frequencies as high as 35,000 cycles per second (Hz), compared to an upper limit of 20,000 Hz for humans. The ability to hear high-pitched sounds accounts for why dogs are able to detect incoming shells before soldiers can. Dogs have an inner ear which they can close, allowing them to filter out background noise and to focus specifically on the task at hand. Those with large erect ears that perk up can hear better than dogs with floppy ears, which is one of the reasons why German shepherds are considered better than other breeds for scout work.

Dogs are actually nearsighted, and don't see as well as humans do in daylight. But at night, their vision is superior to their masters' because within their eyes there are more rods than cones, which respond better to dim light. Also, a dog's eye contains a membrane which reflects light through the retina twice, giving the dog two chances to process the same image.

A breed's temperament, as well as its physiology, influences whether it makes a good war dog. Doberman pinschers were at first the preferred dog for the Marines during World War II. During the course of the war, however, the military changed its emphasis from training sentry and messenger dogs to training scout dogs. While Dobermans were excellent sentries, the Marines soon discovered that they were too excitable and nervous on the battlefield. It took more time for a handler to keep a Doberman calm and under control than it was worth. German shepherds eventually emerged as the first choice for combat dogs because of their more stable temperament. Although bloodhounds have extremely strong scenting ability, the military stopped using them as tracker dogs because they were so noisy. Their baying and barking would have alerted anyone, negating their usefulness in finding the enemy. In the Vietnam War, Labrador retrievers were chosen as tracker dogs because they could be trained to be quiet.

Another consideration is how well dogs stand up to climatic conditions in a country where war is being waged. The sled dogs used in Alaska and Greenland at the beginning of World War II were mostly Siberians and Malamutes, who were able to navigate through snow and withstand the cold. White dogs were chosen so that they could blend into the snow in case commando operations were necessary.

Tropical climates presented severe challenges to most dogs, including heat exhaustion and dehydration. A scout dog handler for the 47th Infantry Platoon Scout Dogs (IPSD) in Vietnam described the following incident in a letter home:

"Yesterday morning we took our dogs out to scout for a while (only practice). They were not out too long and it did not seem that hot but the dogs were really having a rough time of it. We almost lost Trooper. Trooper got so hot that he literally fell down and could not stand up. By the time we got him back to LZ Sally, he still had a temperature of 107 and that was after he had been in the shade and we had poured water over him. Our Vet Tech says that we can expect to lose quite a few dogs due to heat stroke."

German shepherds adapted more easily than most breeds to the heat because they were able to shed their undercoat of fur. This same undercoat meant that they could also adapt well to cold weather. Their versatility is one of the reasons why German shepherds are the most popular breed of war dog.

SORTER

The earliest proof we have that dogs have played a part in warfare for thousands of years is the story of Sorter, a sentry dog. During a battle in the Peloponnesian War (431-404 BC), between the rival Greek city states of Athens and Sparta, the Corinthians had put fifty guard dogs in kennels to guard the shoreline near the citadel of Corinth. The dogs had been trained to stay put, but they had not been chained. One dark night, as the Corinthians lay asleep after a night of drinking, a flotilla of Athenians silently landed on the beach. They crept ashore so silently and so quickly that not a single Corinthian heard them as they prepared to assault the city. But the war dogs heard and quickly attacked, leaping at the soldiers with open jaws. Although they fought ferociously, the armed men had the advantage, and soon all but one dog was killed –

Sorter. We don't know whether Sorter was a coward and hightailed it to town out of fear, or if he simply was smart enough to decide to warn his masters instead. He disobeyed his orders to stay put, and raced into town. There, by barking and pulling officers with his teeth, he roused the Corinthians, who defeated the Athenians.

The grateful soldiers built a monument with Sorter's name, and the names of his fallen comrades, on it. Sorter received a collar, which read, "Sorter, Defender and Saviour of Corinth."

SIR PEERS LEGH'S MASTIFF

The Mastiff, a giant, short-haired dog with a heavy head and short muzzle, has been bred in England as a watchdog for over 2,000 years. Caesar was impressed enough to write about them in his account of his battle with Britain, and Chaucer described their majestic size and power in the *Knight's Tale*.

But the most famous mastiff belonged to Sir Peers Legh, Knight of Lyme Hall (near Stockport, Cheshire). The dog and Sir Peers traveled with King Henry V in 1415 to France to fight the Battle of Agincourt. Though the English won the battle, Sir Peers fell wounded. The mastiff stood over her master, defending him for many hours until he was picked up by his comrades and taken to Paris. When Sir Peers died of his wounds, the dog was taken back to England.

Still at Lyme Hall today is a stained glass window in the drawing room portraying the gallant knight and his devoted dog. The present-day English mastiff breed is based on the strain of mastiff from Lyme Hall.

NAPOLEON BONAPARTE REMEMBERS

Dogs were often taken along as mascots during the Napoleonic Wars (1800–15). One such dog was immortalized when Napoleon Bonaparte wrote about him in his memoirs. The dog sat beside his dead master at the Battle of Marengo in Italy, trying futilely to rouse him. When that failed, the dog repeatedly tried to bring Napoleon over to the corpse, sensing that perhaps Napoleon, of all men, could do something. Napoleon wrote:

> "This soldier, I realized, must have had friends at home and in his regiment; yet he lay there deserted by all except his dog...I had looked on, unmoved, at battles which decided the future of nations. Tearless, I had given orders which brought death to thousands. Yet, here I was stirred, profoundly stirred, stirred to tears. And by what? By the grief of one dog..."

MOUSTACHE, A BLACK FRENCH POODLE

Another dog, a black poodle named Moustache, started as the pet of a regiment of French Grenadiers in the Austrian campaign during the Napoleonic Wars. But Moustache quickly became more than a mascot. One night in 1800, while the troops slept near the Valley of Babo in Italy, Moustache suddenly started to bark. The soldiers awoke just in time to fight off a surprise attack from the Austrians. Another day, a messenger entered the camp. To the men's puzzlement, Moustache growled and snarled at the messenger, and eventually had to be restrained from attacking him. After the messenger left camp, it was discovered that he had been no messenger at all, but, in fact, a spy. Moustache was sent to track him down, and helped capture the man.

Moustache's most heroic act came during the Battle of Austerlitz, an especially difficult battle for the French. Moustache went to the rescue of a young French flag-bearer, who lay dying. The ensign, bearing the regimental colors, had tried to save the flag by wrapping it around his

A Black Poodle

body. Moustache couldn't save the soldier, so instead he retrieved the flag and bore it triumphantly back to his own lines.

For his daring, Napoleon's field marshal, Lannes, gave Moustache a tricolor collar with a silver medal, which read on one side "Moustache, A French dog, a brave fighter entitled to respect," and on the other "At the Battle of Austerlitz, he had his leg broken while saving the flag of his regiment."

Moustache was later presented to the Emperor Napoleon, who was quite amused when the dog performed his best trick: raising his leg when the Emperor's enemies were mentioned.

WAR DOGS IN EARLY AMERICA

Throughout the early part of the United States' history, dogs were never considered to be an important element in the war arsenal. In fact, the military ignored suggestions by several prominent Americans to train dogs. Both Benjamin Franklin, in 1755, and John Penn, in 1764, suggested that dogs should be used against Indians, both as sentry and attack dogs, but no official action was taken to put their ideas into practice.

The first recorded use of dogs by the U.S. Army was in the Second Seminole War during the 1830s, when Cuban bloodhounds were used to track Indians in the swamps of western Florida and Louisiana. The Indians, who knew the dense underbrush and swamps of their native land like the backs of their hands, were effectively using the terrain to ambush soldiers who were trying to capture them. The bloodhounds' sense of smell and ability to move through the swampland's thick vegetation made them invaluable trackers.

Dogs were not used in the American military again until the Spanish–American War in 1898 in Cuba. The Americans were winning

A BRINDEL BULL TERRIER

handily, except when on horseback patrol in the Cuban jungle. Guerrillas there were able to conceal themselves in the underbrush and surprise the Americans. The commander of one cavalry troop knew what to do: he used a dog named Don on every patrol he made. Not one of the patrols with Don in the lead was ambushed.

Despite these early successes with dogs as sentries and trackers, none of the canines that accompanied American soldiers into battle during the Civil War was a formally trained war dog. Most were family dogs, raised on the farm, whom their loving masters couldn't bear to leave behind. Despite their lack of preparation for the horrors of war, many displayed great loyalty and courage.

SALLIE, A BRINDEL BULL TERRIER

One Civil War mascot was Sallie, a brindel bull terrier who joined the 11th Pennsylvania Voluntary Infantry at the start of the war and traveled with them to Gettysburg, Pennsylvania. On July 1, 1863, on the first day of battle and in steaming heat, Sallie took up her position with her unit on the Union battle line atop Oak Ridge, barking as loudly as she could at the Confederates.

But the 11th Voluntary unit was forced to retreat. They fled into town, following the railroad tracks towards the west. Somehow, as the men ran over the corn fields, Sallie became separated from her unit. Refusing to pass through Rebel lines, she returned to Oak Ridge and stayed with the fallen Union men, licking their wounds and guarding the dead. Days after the battle was over and the Confederates had retreated, a Union soldier from the 12th Massachusetts Infantry found Sallie, who was by then weak with hunger. Later, back with her unit, Sallie nabbed a frightened soldier from a different regiment who was running away from the battle line when he unfortunately chose to cross Sallie's path.

Sallie died two years later at the battle of Hatcher's Run, Virginia, from a bullet wound. At Gettysburg today, there is a statue honoring the heroic dead of the 11th Pennsylvania Voluntary Infantry. Another statue, at the front base of the 11th Pennsylvania memorial, honors Sallie, a small, brave mascot of the Civil War.

LT. PFIEFF'S DOG

Another Civil War Union dog was at the battle of Shiloh in Tennessee in April, 1862, with his master, Lt. Louis Pfieff of the 3rd Illinois Infantry. Lt. Pfieff was one of 20,000 casualties during two days of fierce fighting, and when his widow came days later to claim the body, she searched for hours among thousands of hastily dug graves. No one could tell her where her husband lay. As the sun sank, the grief-ridden Mrs. Pfieff was about to give up when she saw her husband's dog coming toward her. Mrs. Pfieff was overjoyed to see him, and he greeted Mrs. Pfieff warmly. Then the dog started to move away from her, looking over his shoulder, as if he wanted to lead her somewhere. Sure enough, he led her to where her husband was buried in a distant part of the field. The dog had stood watch over the grave for 12 days, leaving only to get food and water.

BRITISH HONOREES

By the mid-1800s, dogs were being included for citations with the medals being handed out to brave British soldiers. The Victoria Cross was instituted by Queen Victoria in 1856 as a way of rewarding the bravery of enlisted men and lower ranking officers. There were 522 Victoria Crosses awarded up to World War I, and some of the awards include mention of dogs. The King and Queen South Africa Medal, given to soldiers serving in South Africa in 1901 and 1902, also honored dogs as well as men.

DICK, A FOX TERRIER

Things were looking bad for the British 24th Foot in January, 1879, during the Zulu Wars in South Africa. The Zulus had annihilated several companies that day, and were looking for their next target. The

A WIRE-HAIRED FOX TERRIER

B Company, 2nd Battalion, 24th Regiment, were holding a farm at Rorke's Drift. Fortunately, they had been alerted to the danger of attack by a soldier who had escaped an earlier massacre.

At 4:30 p.m., 5,000 Zulu warriors descended on the farm buildings, including the barn which was being used as the hospital. Surgeon James Henry Reynolds and his fox terrier Dick ignored the fighting and concentrated on caring for the injured. Eventually, the Zulus set fire to the hospital, and Reynolds and his men moved the wounded out into the open. Dick never wavered, as shots and spears continued falling all around. He only left his master's side to bite a Zulu who came too close. The Zulus retreated some 12 hours later. Surgeon Reynolds received the Victoria Cross for his bravery. Dick was specially mentioned in the citation for "his constant attention to the wounded under fire where they fell."

SCOUT

The Royal Dragoons were on their way to fight in the Boer War in South Africa in 1899. Their troopship, the SS *Manchester Port*, sailed into Durban, Natal, on November 26. As the soldiers began to eat, a puppy began nosing around, and happily settled down when the men began sharing their food. She showed up again next morning, but the men had already upped anchor and set sail upriver for Pietermaritzburg. Somehow, she managed to hop on a train bound for the same place, and was reunited with the Royal Dragoons. She quickly established herself as always being at the head of the parade, and so the men named her Scout. Her first battle was the Battle of Colenso, where she was put on patrol duty. She acted as a guard dog at the Battle of Spion Kop. When peace was declared, Scout marched at the head of the regiment, and again she led the way when the Royal Dragoons went to Cape Town to embark for England. Scout earned both the Queen and King South Africa Medals for her heroism.

Chapter Two

Allied Dogs Lead the Way: World War I

WAR DOG TRAINING BEGINS

Europeans began formally training dogs for war at the end of the nineteenth century. Perhaps they began formal war dog training earlier than Americans did because of the long tradition on the Continent of taking dogs into battle. There were reports in 1895 of Germans buying sheep dogs from Scottish shepherds for the purpose of training them for the German army. In 1905, Airedales were used by the Russians in the Russo-Japanese war to pull ambulance sleds. Lieutenant Dupin of the 32nd French Infantry began testing dogs for military purposes in 1906, and by 1915 the French military had established the Service des Chiens de Guerre. And Edwin H. Richardson, a gentleman farmer in England, was training dogs for war well before World War I broke out.

But the beginning of World War I in 1914 brought the first large-scale effort in history by many countries to train dogs for specific duties in war. By 1918, Italy had trained about 3,500 war dogs, France and England had 20,000 war dogs, and Germany had 30,000. The United States was the only country that did not consider dogs an important asset in fighting the Great War.

Dogs had been used on the battlefield for hundreds of years, but they were especially useful during World War I because of the nature of warfare at that time. World War I was fought very differently from previous or subsequent wars. Soldiers, for instance, spent long periods of time in trenches in battle lines that sometimes didn't move for weeks. Between opponents battle lines, there was a barren expanse of land that exposed soldiers to enemy fire. Dogs, however, with their low profile and four-legged speed, could accomplish things in this no-man's-land that humans could not.

Perhaps the most widely used kind of trained dog was the mercy dog, who was taught to help find and bring back wounded soldiers. Sentry dogs gave their masters in the trenches advance warning of the enemy, and prevented foes from getting close enough to throw hand grenades. Messenger dogs carried dispatches over barbed wire, trenches and even through chemical gas.

MERCY DOGS

During World War I, every country had its own Red Cross institution and, with the exception of the United States, used mercy dogs extensively to help find and comfort the wounded. Under the cover of night, dogs would hunt for injured men in no-man's-land, carrying water and medicines to them, and then would head back to camp to alert their masters. The dogs would then lead stretcher bearers back to the injured, so they could be carried back to safety. Mercy dogs were trained specifically not to bark so they wouldn't alert the enemy. Many of the breeds trained for this task were innate retrievers, and would bring a cap or helmet to signal to their masters that they had found a wounded man.

One French dog named Prusco found more than a hundred wounded men after a single battle. According to a 1917 issue of *Red Cross Magazine* Prusco also often dragged these wounded soldiers into craters and trenches to protect them.

The several thousand mercy dogs who served in World War I saved countless lives and undoubtedly were as heroic as messengers or sentries, yet there are few stories about particular mercy dogs. Probably this is because mercy dogs weren't trained to serve individual masters like messengers or sentries were.

Instead, a mercy dog would silently walk among the wounded, who may or may not have been aware of the role the dog played in saving their lives. Even if the soldiers were able to notice, they were usually taken off the field and sent somewhere else for treatment so that they never saw the dog again.

An American surgeon, Malcolm C. Grow, who fought with the Russians during World War I, painted in his autobiography a vivid portrait of the role mercy dogs played. His book entitled *Surgeon Grow: An American In the Russian Fighting*, was published in 1918 by Frederick A. Stokes. Below is an extract from Grow's book, about Airedales that were used on the Russian front.

An Airedale Terrier

A Story About Three Airedale Mercy Dogs

"We had with us three Airedale terriers. They were trained to locate the wounded in thickets and brushy places where they could not be seen by our searching parties, who, for obvious reasons, could not carry any light.

"About two o'clock we received word that a wounded man had managed to crawl in from between the lines and had reported that some badly wounded soldiers were lying in a thicket and were perishing in the cold. He had passed several of them as he crawled painfully by. They were too weak to move but displayed signs of life.

"I summoned the three orderlies who had charge of the dogs, and, taking twelve stretcher-bearers, hurried to our trenches opposite the point indicated. The weather had moderated slightly and the snow was melting a little, but it was one of those damp, penetrating nights when the cold seems to go right through to the bone.

"As we splashed through a communication trench, the dogs tugging at their leashes, I thought of those poor devils lying out there, suffering all kinds of anguish and without any hope of being rescued.

"It was as dark as a pit as we entered the first-line trenches. They were full of soldiers sitting about shivering in the cold and waiting for the next order to attack.

"In the occasional flicker of a rocket, I could make out, halfway between our trenches and the Germans, a dark patch of scrubby weeds and stunted bushes. In this little thicket lay the wounded.

"The orderlies who had charge of the dogs lifted them up on the parapet, unsnapped their leashes, and spoke a sharp word of command:
'Begone!'

"The dogs disappeared in the darkness of No Man's Land and were gone for quite a long time. I thought at first that they must have gone astray or that one of those scattering volleys from the German trenches had ended their mission of rescue.

"Tang!

"Something in our entanglements had struck a projecting piece of wire directly in front of me. A rocket shot up, and over the parapet a yard to my right I saw a shaggy head peering down. The dog held something in his mouth. I heard him whine softly. One of the orderlies reached up to get him and he snarled savagely and jumped back. It was not his master and he was trained when on duty to keep away from any other person.

"Another orderly stepped up on the firestep and spoke to him, and he whimpered softly and came to his master, who lifted him down. In the light of my electric torch I saw that he held in his mouth a crumpled, blood-stained cap. His master took the cap in his hand, snapped the leash on the dog's collar, lifted him up on the parapet and crawled up after him, followed by two stretcher-bearers.

"The dog led them out through the barbed wire, tugging at his leash, and I followed the little party, curious to see whether he would find the owner of that cap.

"I could distinguish their dim forms as they crawled on hands and knees, dragging the rolled-up stretcher after them. I followed, also crawling, and when a rocket soared up and cast its ghostly light over the field, we all 'froze,' lying perfectly flat in the snow until the light died out.

"I heard the dry grass crackle as they wormed their way into the thicket and I thought that we must be very close to the German lines. Several bullets struck the weeds about me.

"My hand touched something which felt like a piece of woolen cloth in the weeds and I saw a dark object lying partly concealed in the thicket. I reached out and felt a human arm – it was hard and stiff and the clutched hand was icy. I tried to move the arm, but it was rigid and I knew that there was no life in that cold body.

"I crawled hurriedly on through the bush and found the little party kneeling about another dark object sprawled in the snow. The body was still warm but the hands were very cold and at the wrist I could feel only a tiny trickle of pulse. I passed my hand up to his head. The cap was gone and the hair was stiff and matted with frozen blood, but just above the ear I felt a warm moist spot. I knew that this was the wounded point and that the fresh blood was oozing forth. The bullet had entered the brain and the soldier was unconscious, but it was evidently the man whose cap the dog had brought to our trenches.

"One of the orderlies had a first aid kit, and we hurriedly put on a dressing to keep the dirt out. We slid him on to the stretcher and started back, crawling and dragging the stretcher after us.

"Our progress was necessarily very slow, for with each rocket we had to lie quiet. The German trenches were not more than forty yards away. Finally, however, we reached our wire and passed through one of the lanes which had been cut to let the attacking waves through.

"The stretcher was carefully passed down to waiting hands below, and the wounded man wrapped in blankets, and we started back for the dressing station. I learned that the other two dogs had returned in the meantime, one with a cap and the other with a piece of cloth ripped by his fangs from a wounded man's overcoat. The dogs are trained to tear something from the soldier's garments if they cannot find a cap or glove. Whatever the dog brings back is used to refresh its memory when the rescue party starts after the wounded man, the orderly passing it across the animal's nose whenever he falters.

"One of the rescue parties returned with an abdominal case, a bad one, so weak that I could scarcely detect a sign of life.

"'Do the dogs ever take you to dead bodies?' I asked the orderly.

" 'No, Excellency, never,' he replied. 'They sometimes lead us to bodies which we think have no life in them, but when we bring them back the doctors, by careful examination, always find a spark though often very feeble. It is purely a matter of instinct, which, in this instance, is far more effective than man's reasoning powers.'

"Presently a third party returned with a man with a broken thigh. He was almost lifeless from exposure and shock.

"So the work went on until we had recovered fourteen wounded. Then one of the dogs returned without anything in his mouth. He was sent back again and while he was gone another returned, also without any 'evidence.' When, after a little while, all three dogs stuck their shaggy heads over the parapet with nothing in their mouths, we were tolerably sure that there were no more wounded Russians in the thicket.

"By that time, the first gray light of dawn was struggling to dispel the night. As I went back to the main dressing station through the ghostly forest, our artillery was pounding furiously at the German lines. Then came the infernal crackle of rifles and the tack! tack! of machine-guns and the flickering of rockets as another wave of our infantry went over the top in a second desperate attack to break the German lines. As I pictured the inrush of the flowing stream of wounded pouring down the road through the forest to our dressing stations, I realized that there would be little rest for me that day."

Thousands of soldiers were rescued by mercy dogs, and many more were comforted in their last hour. A 1918 painting by Alexander Pope, hanging in the Red Cross Museum in Washington, D.C., immortalizes the contribution of these special dogs.

THE BRITISH WAR DOG SCHOOL

The British Army might never have used war dogs if it had not been for the efforts of Edwin H. Richardson. A dog breeder and trainer, Richardson had been interested in dogs ever since he was a young boy.

By the late 1890s, Richardson was traveling in Europe to keep himself in touch with the various dog training schools in France, Germany, Holland and Belgium. He also traveled to Germany, where he wrote in his autobiography that he had discovered "a fine collection of collies, which were training for finding wounded. They wore Red Cross jackets, and were very well broken."

In 1905, Richardson received a wire from the Russian Embassy, asking him to supply ambulance dogs for the Russian troops. His Airedales performed so well that Dowager Empress Marie sent him the Red Cross medal for his help.

Over the next ten years, he sent dogs as far away as Turkey, Spain, and India to serve as ambulance dogs, sentries, and guard dogs.

When war broke out in 1914, Richardson began making efforts to

A BORDER COLLIE

get the British War Department to start a war dog program. While they hemmed and hawed, he offered his ambulance dogs to the Red Cross. He also began sending sentry and messenger dogs to soldiers at the Front who, frustrated by the British War Department's lack of response, had written directly to him requesting the dogs. His dog training operation continued, and finally, in 1917, the War Department asked him to start the British War Dog School. For this, Richardson obtained his first 500 dogs through a War Department request to private citizens and stray dog homes. Dogs were trained in England, then sent to kennels near the front line in France.

A handler would take three dogs at a time and assign each to an infantryman at the Front. In order to help oversee the dogs the handler was based at the brigade's headquarters.

Purebreds and mutts alike were considered suitable for training, and included German shepherds, Airedales, sheepdogs, retrievers, bloodhounds, and bulldogs. Airedales were among the most common and popular breeds, and were eventually named the official breed of the British Army. Medium-sized dogs that were grayish or black were preferred so they could blend into the landscape.

More important than breed, however, were intelligence and character. A dog's disposition was the most important criterion in the field — he had to be loyal and responsive to his master's commands. Richardson was quoted in a newspaper article as saying, "The breed does not matter so much, it is brains that we want."

Early on, Richardson identified some of the key elements that are still used in training war dogs today. Whilst praise was encouraged to reward the dogs during training, soldiers were discouraged from being too friendly when the dogs were working and feeding them while they

A Golden Retriever

were at the Front was forbidden. Without food digesting in their stomachs', the dogs would remain alert, with their minds on the task at hand. Richardson also insisted that dogs shouldn't stay longer than 12 hours on the front line, because after that they became too hungry and tired to work effectively.

A newspaper reporter gave the following account of a visit to the British War Dog Training School:

"The drill began with an obstacle race by a squad well advanced in training. Across the road were placed a barbed wire fence and a few yards further on a hurdle, and beyond that a barrier made of branches of trees. The dogs were taken about a mile up the road and then released. There was a great race for home. The bigger dogs leapt clear of all the obstructions; the smaller ones wriggled their way through... The dogs are trained to ignore the fire of guns of all calibers, and they are accustomed to the explosion of hand grenades near them... Then the next test for the dogs was passing through a thick cloud of smoke. They were released only a few yards away from a burning heap of straw, and all, without a pause, dashed straight through the smoke and reached their destination with much barking and tail wagging... Novices who go astray in these and other tests are never never punished. They are caught by the keepers and gently led back for another try."

Apparently the training worked well, for there are several British hero dogs who became famous in World War I.

AIREDALE JACK

As did many of England's first fighting dogs, Airedale Jack came from the Battersea Dogs Home in London, a shelter for strays. At the British War Dog School, Airedale Jack was taught to be a messenger and a sentry and, in 1918, he was sent over to France.

The Sherwood Foresters took Airedale Jack to an advance post at the Front. There, the battle raged, and the Germans succeeded in cutting off every line of communication with headquarters, which was four miles behind the lines.

Unless reinforcements were secured, it was certain that the entire battalion would be wiped out. It was impossible for any man to get through the barrage of gunfire.

There was just one chance – Airedale Jack. Lieutenant Hunter slipped a message into the leather pouch attached to the dog's collar. "Good-bye Jack . . . Go back, boy," said Hunter. Jack slipped quietly away toward headquarters, staying close to the ground and taking advantage of whatever cover there was, as he had been trained to do. The bombardment was too heavy, though, and he started to get hit. A piece of shrapnel smashed his jaw, and the battalion watched him stagger on. Another missile ripped open his black and tan coat from shoulder to thigh. Still, he continued forward, using shell-craters and trenches for cover. His forepaw was then hit, and still Jack dragged himself along the ground on three legs for the last few miles. He persevered until he reached headquarters, where he fell dead. He had done a hero's work and saved the battalion.

In the British Imperial War Museum is a small wooden stand which has inscribed on it, "...to the memory of Airedale Jack, a hero of the

Great War." He was presented with a posthumous Victoria Cross, for "Gallantry in the Field."

RELUCTANCE TO ACCEPT WAR DOGS

Sometimes, training the dogs was easier than teaching the soldiers how to use them effectively. Even the French who had a long history of using dogs in battle, counted non-believers in their ranks. One French captain was offered two Alsatian sheep dogs named Za and Helda, but he refused to put them to work. However, Sergeant Paul Megnin, chief of the Service des Chiens de Geurre insisted, and eventually the captain agreed to a test. If the dogs could find a hidden enemy outpost that the captain's troops had been searching for, then the dogs could serve as sentries. That very night, the two dogs sniffed out the enemy only 250 yards from French lines. They went to work as sentries the following day.

In England, the same prejudices held true. Richardson, in his autobiography, writes, "Commanding officers of those battalions to whom they were first sent very often made light of the dogs, or else ignored them, or worse still rather cynically set them to tasks under impossible conditions." Another entry states:

"Definite orders from headquarters were after a time formulated, governing the reception and disposal of these valuable animals, and the men who were responsible for them, so that respect was soon inculcated and was retained, when it was found what could be accomplished by their aid...It was only when the importance of the work which the dogs were able to do began to be realized and it was lifted out of the rut of a rather amused and condescending tolerance, that general officers, officers and men combined to observe in every way, in their own interest, the rules which governed these canine soldiers in their arduous work."

MESSENGER DOGS

Dogs provided a vital communications link during World War I, when rudimentary technology meant that communications often broke down. When soldiers in the front lines were cut off from their colleagues to the rear, they relied on messenger dogs to relay their position and need for reinforcements. Dogs were four to five times faster than humans, and had a lower profile, making it more difficult for the enemy to shoot them. At one battle near Verdun, 17 men were killed attempting to deliver messages, while a single dog completed seven runs before being shot. Dogs could also carry messenger pigeons in special saddle bags designed specifically for that purpose.

SATAN: MESSENGER DOG

Satan, a black mixed breed, is the most famous messenger dog of World War I because he saved hundreds of French soldiers who were surrounded by Germans and fighting for their lives. Satan performed his act of heroism in 1916 in France during the Battle of Verdun, which had been going on for months. French troops had taken and lost a small but strategically important town called Thiaumont sixteen times.

This time, several hundred Frenchmen occupied the garrison at Thiaumont, but were surrounded by German forces. The French soldiers were running out of ammunition, their telephone lines were cut, and their messenger pigeons were dead. The Germans were shelling the falling garrison relentlessly. With no ammunition and dwindling supplies of food, French soldiers were dying or being wounded at an alarming rate. Worst of all, no one at French headquarters in Verdun knew of their plight – and headquarters was only two miles away!

Most of the damage was being done by a German artillery unit that occupied a nearby hill. The French soldiers knew that if reinforcements could stop the barrage from the artillery unit, they might have a chance. But they had no way of communicating with headquarters. Soldiers had tried to run through enemy lines, and failed. And their messenger dog, Satan, was at headquarters, on the wrong side of enemy lines.

Fortunately, officers in Verdun began to suspect that something was wrong. They hadn't heard from Thiaumont in days. They also heard the constant gunfire, and knew that the French supply of ammunition couldn't have lasted so long. They decided that Satan had the best chance of getting a message to the soldiers at the front.

Satan had already shown himself to be fearless during previous runs through enemy fire. His father, a champion English greyhound, had endowed him with speed, and his working Scotch collie mother had passed along her intelligence. Most of all, Satan loved his master, Duval, who was back in Thiaumont. Duval was a well-known dog trainer from the War Dog School at Satory. He had joined the battalion with two dogs, Satan and Rip. But Rip, an Irish setter, had already been killed in action.

Officers inserted a message into the metal canister attached to Satan's collar, strapped two carrier pigeons into a harness on his back, and put a soldier's gas mask over his muzzle to protect him from gas.

For the first mile and a half, Satan traveled carefully, crouching close to the ground and taking cover behind shrubs and hummocks. When he came in sight of the garrison, the terrain opened up, and there was no longer any cover to hide behind. Satan began to run in a zigzag, as he had been trained to do to avoid being shot. Meanwhile, the Germans caught sight of him, and rained gunfire on him from all sides.

Through the smoke, Duval and other soldiers at the garrison caught sight of something running toward them, but at first they couldn't figure out what it was. The gas mask and pigeon carriers made Satan look like a large-headed, winged beast. Satan kept running until, just several hundred yards short of the French line, a German bullet hit him. He fell, but got up again, and continued more slowly. Another bullet hit him in the shoulder, and this time he became disoriented and unsure, with one leg swinging loose at the hip.

Satan's master, Duval, stood up and called out to Satan, urging him on. Duval went down after a bullet hit him, but Satan made the last few steps into waiting French arms. The message from headquarters read, "For God's sake, hold on! Will send troops to relieve you tomorrow."

An officer quickly wrote a message back detailing the artillery unit's position and requesting help immediately. He copied the message onto a second piece of paper, and put each message into the capsule attached to each pigeon's leg. Everyone watched as the first pigeon took off toward headquarters. It flew only 300 yards before it was shot down. The second pigeon took off amid a hail of bullets, but they didn't see it fall.

Within 20 minutes, long-range French guns began shooting toward the artillery unit on the hill. The French won Thiaumont that same day – all because Satan had shown the courage to keep going. Satan recovered from his leg injury and retired from the French Army a hero.

Chapter Three

American Mascot Dogs: World War I

ILL-FATED EFFORTS

Unlike Europe, where dogs were considered an important asset when waging war, the United States never formally decided to use dogs during World War I, despite many recommendations to the contrary. When the U.S. entered World War I in 1917, both the German Shepherd Dog Club of America and the Army and Police Dog Club of the United States tried to persuade the military to build up a war dog program. In 1918, the General Headquarters of the American Expeditionary Force recommended that 500 dogs be obtained from the French every three months, with training to be done at newly established facilities in the United States. With the example of successful European war dogs all around them at the Front, it is surprising that the U.S. military ignored these suggestions.

Even private citizens got in on the act. Wanting to help their country, many people donated dogs to the American Red Cross to be used as mercy dogs. But the effort was ill-fated.

American dog trainers, despite having the best intentions, had no experience of war and found it difficult to prepare the dogs for the chaos and noise at the Front. Some of the dogs were trained in the country, and couldn't tolerate even the noise of city life. No coordinated method of training them was established, so that dogs were taught different things in different ways. The few dogs that were finally shipped overseas with the Red Cross were virtually useless, because they weren't properly prepared for battle conditions.

Regulations clearly stated that dogs were not allowed in the U.S. military, but the lack of an official war dog program didn't stop soldiers from taking their best friends with them when they shipped out. Mascots traveled with many troops, and, while some performed acts of bravery, many dogs simply stayed by their masters' sides, offering companionship and trust during difficult times. Some of these dogs, though untrained, were clearly suited temperamentally to the extreme conditions of war. In any case, many were so loyal to their masters that nothing else mattered to them. The stories below of Stubby and Rags, two strays adopted by American soldiers, proves how valuable even untrained dogs can be during wartime.

STUBBY, THE HERO DOG

Corporal Robert Conroy was completing his military training in the summer of 1917 in the Yale Bowl in New Haven, Connecticut, when he found Stubby, a stray pit bull. Whether he was named because of his chunky body or his short tail is unclear. Although Stubby wouldn't have

A Pit Bull Terrier

won any beauty contests, his friendliness and constancy did win him many friends. Stubby was there at the Bowl, day after day, as the 102nd Infantry, part of the Army's 26th Division, did their drills. When the division received its orders to move on to final training in Newport News, Virginia, Conroy smuggled Stubby along by hiding him under the equipment in a supply car.

Soon after that, the 102nd shipped out to St. Nazaire, France. The day they were due to leave, Conroy asked a military police officer guarding the ship to help him smuggle Stubby aboard. As was his way, the dog charmed the MP, and Stubby became part of the 102nd when it landed in France in January, 1918. They moved to the Front in February, at Chemin des Dames, just northwest of Soissons.

Stubby was on the front line for the next year and a half, and he participated in 17 battles, including those at Chateau-Thierry, the Marne, Saint-Mihiel, and the Meuse-Argonne. His acute sense of hearing and smell allowed him to sense danger before soldiers could. After arriving at the Front, he quickly learned from the soldiers to head for cover whenever he heard the whine of shells. Since Stubby could hear the high pitched shells before the men could, they began watching him, noting his movements as a kind of early warning system. Soon it became a game to see who could reach the dugout first.

One night while everyone was asleep Stubby smelled poison gas. He began running through the trenches, waking the men with his loud barking, which gave the soldiers time to put on their gas masks. Stubby, however, succumbed to the gas. Conroy took him to the base hospital where he quickly recovered. Later, Conroy tried to fashion a mask for him, but couldn't manage to fit one around Stubby's blunt nose. Gas masks for dogs weren't issued by the American military until World War II.

On another occasion, in the dead of night, Stubby woke Conroy up by growling quietly. Then the dog took off, and Conroy grabbed his rifle and followed. Lieutenant Conroy could hear a struggle, and then a loud cry. He came upon Stubby, with his mouth firmly clamped onto the seat of a German infiltrator. Conroy disarmed the German, but had a tougher time persuading Stubby to let go of his catch.

Stubby received his most serious injury in the Toul sector, where he strayed too close to the enemy. A hand grenade landed a few feet away from him, leaving him with a shrapnel wound which nearly killed him. But he recovered, and six weeks later was back at the Front with his troop.

As Stubby participated in battle after battle, and recovered from countless mishaps, his popularity and notoriety grew. The men made a Victory Medal for him, and attached it to his collar. Several French women made a blanket coat for him, and people began pinning Allied flags and medals on it. This was when Stubby became known as the Hero Dog. Stubby even got a medal for saving a civilian. One day, when he and Conroy were on a walk in Paris, Stubby suddenly bolted toward a girl standing on the sidewalk. He lunged upward and knocked her aside, just before an out-of-control taxi would have hit her.

Stubby returned home to the United States in 1919, where his popularity continued to grow. The Eastern Dog Club of Boston gave him a silver medal in 1920, and in 1921 General John J. Pershing awarded Stubby a gold medal made by the Humane Society. The American Red Cross, the YMCA, and the American Legion made Stubby a lifetime member. The YMCA also gave Stubby a membership card for "three bones a day and a place to sleep." Three American presidents – Woodrow Wilson, Warren G. Harding, and Calvin Coolidge – met Stubby. He led parades, and he toured the U.S. with the Legionnaires. When Conroy went to Georgetown

Law School in 1921, Stubby became mascot of the football team. He was even allowed to check into a New York City hotel where dogs were not allowed, because he was Stubby, the Hero Dog.

Stubby became an icon because of his ability to survive and because of his loyalty at all costs. His acts of bravery were many and small, but they added up – setting an example for soldiers and civilians alike.

Stubby died of old age in 1926, in Conroy's arms. A curator at the American Red Cross museum asked for his body so that it could be exhibited at the museum. A taxidermist then made a plaster mold of Stubby's body, and stretched his skin around it. Adorned with his French blanket covered with medals, Stubby stood in his glass case for nearly 30 years. Unfortunately, his skin started eroding, and the Smithsonian's Museum of American History took possession of the memorial, which is no longer on public view.

RAGS, A BRAVE MUTT

All that remains of Rags is a small grave at Aspen Hill Memorial Park, a pet cemetery in Silver Spring, Maryland. The tombstone reads, "RAGS, War Hero, 1st Division Mascot, WWI 1916–1936." But this small, shaggy mutt, picked up by an American soldier off the streets of Paris, led a heroic life and made many friends along the way.

Private James Donovan, of the American 1st Infantry Division, was wandering through Paris on the evening of July 14, 1918 – Bastille Day. He stumbled over what appeared to be a pile of rags. Just as Donovan realized it was a dog, three Military Police officers arrived, and asked to see his pass. Donovan, who was officially A.W.O.L, thought fast. He had been searching for the 1st Division's mascot dog, he fibbed. He picked up the dog, who he quickly dubbed Rags, and displayed him for the MPs to see. The MPs bought Donovan's story, and escorted both soldier and dog back to Donovan's unit.

There, Donovan learned that he and his captain were moving to division headquarters at the Front to establish a new communication link between infantry and artillery units. His job was to string and repair communications wire between advancing infantry units of the 26th Infantry Regiment and the supporting 7th Field Artillery Brigade during the Battle of the Marne.

Rags insisted on following Donovan through the trenches, despite Donovan's efforts to leave him back at headquarters where it was safer. So, Donovan decided to put Rags to use.

When shellfire cut the communications wire, and runners couldn't get through, Donovan taught Rags to take messages back to the 7th Field Artillery. Rags followed the sound of American gunfire to run toward the artillery unit, and he had no trouble finding Donovan with return messages.

In late July, 1918, however, Rags was put to the test. During a counterattack driving toward the Paris-Soissons road, Rags and Donovan found themselves caught with an artillery unit that was surrounded by Germans. The only surviving officer, a young lieutenant, wrote the following message and attached it to Rags' collar: "I have forty-two men, mixed, healthy and wounded. We have advanced to the road but can go no farther. Most of the men are from the 26th Infantry. I am the only officer. Machine guns at our rear, front, right, and left. Send infantry officer to take command. I need machine gun ammunition."

Rags took off, through barbed wire, over trenches, unseen by the Germans. He made it back to the 7th Field Artillery, where the message was given to headquarters. An artillery barrage began, and reinforcements soon rescued the stranded unit. That day, Rags became a hero among the men of the 1st Infantry Division.

After the Marne fighting, Donovan and Rags had a chance to rest. Donovan fitted Rags with a special gas mask, specially suited for his nose. Donovan also taught Rags to salute, by lifting his paw just a little higher and closer to his head than he would have to shake hands. The story soon spread that Rags had saluted Major General Charles P. Summerall, the new Commanding Officer of the 1st Division, who had a reputation of being a most demanding general. During this rest time, Rags also began touring mess halls, looking for the most delectable fare and the friendliest soldiers. During one tour, Rags took issue with a cat, who happened to belong to a division staff officer named Col. Theodore Roosevelt, Jr. Rags' mess hall perambulations were curtailed shortly thereafter.

Rags served not only as a messenger dog. Like Stubby, Rags could hear shells well before human ears could, and the soldiers quickly learned to follow his lead in seeking cover.

Rags also fought in hand-to-hand combat alongside Donovan, during the first all-American offensive of the war in September, 1918. At the beginning of the four-day drive to eliminate the St. Michel salient, the Germans began an immediate retreat. Fighting was mostly hand-to-hand as advancing American infantrymen caught up with retreating Germans. Twice, Donovan went head-on for Germans as Rags "barked, snarled, and grabbed German legs with his teeth."

During the final American campaign of World War I, at the Meuse–Argonne, Donovan and Rags were again responsible for keeping the communication lines open between the 26th Infantry and 7th Field

Artillery. German resistance was strong, and Rags carried messages to the artillery unit several times. On October 2nd, he took the following message to the unit:

"From C.O. 1st Bn. 26th Infantry, Oct. 2 – 12:30
To Captain Thomas, Intelligence Officer:
Have artillery that is firing in small, oblong-shaped woods, directly in front and on right of first objective, lengthen range and pound hell out of the woods. Machine gun nests are located there.
Legge, Cdg."

The artillery found its mark, and the 26th Infantry secured its objective.

A week later, in the Argonne Forest, Donovan and Rags were to fight their last fight. Amid dense fog, the 26th Infantry division were preparing for a German attack. Communication lines were down, and the fog and terrain made it impossible to see clearly. Rags was sent back to the 2nd Battalion of the 7th Field Artillery without his gas mask, but bearing a message. However, the Germans began firing gas shells, followed by an artillery barrage and fragments of an exploding shell cut Rags' forepaw, injured his right ear and a needle-like sliver pierced his right eye. He continued on, but a second round of fire dazed him. A soldier found Rags and delivered him to the artillery unit. Meanwhile, Donovan was severely gassed and then wounded by shellfire as he was carried to the rear. Rags was placed on Donovan's stretcher, and both were taken behind the lines.

Rags and Donovan were treated side-by-side for their injuries. When anyone questioned why a dog would be given treatment equal to a soldier's care, someone would defend Rags by saying it was "orders from headquarters." Early on, it was assumed that the 1st Division Commanding Officer was giving these orders, but with time people began to assume the command was coming from General John Pershing himself. Rags' paw healed and he gradually improved, although he was blind in his right eye and deaf in his right ear.

Donovan did not recover as well from his gas-damaged lungs, and soon received orders to be shipped home as soon as possible. An injured colonel smuggled Rags aboard the hospital boat with Donovan, and men of the 1st Division kept Rags hidden and fed during the journey home. When the pair arrived in Hoboken, New Jersey, Rags was again smuggled aboard the train that took Donovan to Fort Sheridan, in Chicago.

At Fort Sheridan, Rags settled into ways that endeared him to everyone. He became so well known that the fort commander had a collar made for him which read "1st Division Rags." Each morning, he would wait outside the front door of the hospital until a soldier would take him for a visit with Donovan. Then he would wander the grounds, stopping at mess halls to see what was good to eat. In the evenings, he attended the retreat ceremony, which included firing the cannon, playing the bugle, and lowering the flag. Then it was off to bed at the firehouse, where he slept beneath a hose cart.

In 1919, Donovan died. But every morning, Rags continued to show up at the hospital door. Finally, someone had the idea of showing Rags Donovan's empty bed, after which he stopped coming to the hospital.

Early in 1920, Rags adopted new masters, Major Raymond W. Hardenberg and his family, when they were transferred to Fort Sheridan. Hardenberg had two daughters, and Rags and the girls immediately liked one another. Rags began accompanying the girls to school and staying for dinner and, eventually, he moved in with the family.

Rags traveled with the Hardenbergs as they were transferred to various posts. At Fort Benning, he was hit by a car, but he soon recovered. In 1924, Major Hardenberg was transferred to Governor's Island in New York Harbor, where various 1st Division troops were stationed. Many soldiers were familiar with the story of Rags, and he quickly re-established himself as the 1st Division mascot. In addition to roaming the mess halls and the island at large, Rags took to riding the ferries that traveled to Fort Hamilton, Fort Wadsworth, and Battery Park.

By 1926, Rags had become a celebrity. In October, he was given an award honoring his wartime achievements at the Long Island Kennel Club dog show. A book and several magazine articles about him appeared. As an important part of the 1st Division's 10th reunion in 1928, he marched in a parade down Broadway, and participated in a battle re-enactment at Fort Hamilton. He then had his picture taken with the man he had allegedly saluted during World War I, and who was now 1st Division Commander Summerall, a four-star general, along with several other former division commanders. In 1931, he was inducted into the Legion of Dog Heroes by the New York Anti-Vivisection Society.

Rags lived the rest of his life at Fort Hamilton and in Washington, D.C., with the Hardenberg family. He died in 1936 at the age of 20. *The New York Times* even wrote about his death. Although the 1st Division considered a military burial and monument for him at Fort Hamilton, apparently this never happened.

THE END OF WORLD WAR I

Most of the dogs used in World War I did not enjoy the longevity of Rags. Although it is difficult to count the losses, a 1917 issue of

Animals magazine estimated that seven thousand dogs were killed during the war – probably a low estimate given the total number of dogs used by all of the countries involved. Equally difficult to calculate is the number of lives these war dogs saved – but clearly the number of soldiers who avoided ambush, enemy fire, capture, and death through the work of their canine friends is in the thousands.

Sadly, more dogs probably lost their lives after the war than during it. The French military destroyed all fifteen thousand dogs in their Service des Chiens de Guerre when the war was over. Most dogs used by the British, Germans, Italians and Russians were also killed.

But Americans had begun to notice and appreciate dogs as a result of the war. Whereas before the war, very few people buried their animals, between 1914 and 1917 more dogs were buried at the Hartsdale Pet Cemetery in Hartsdale, New York, than in the previous 20 years.

In 1918, a group decided to build a statue in Hartsdale commemorating history's brave war dogs. Contributions poured in, and a majestic ten-foot high granite monument was created. At the top is a bronze German shepherd wearing a Red Cross blanket. Now, every Memorial Day a ceremony is held to honor the brave dogs that have helped men during wartime.

Chapter Four

Para Pups and Anti-Tank Dogs: World War II

A SLOW START FOR BRITISH WAR DOGS

Despite the lessons learned concerning the value of dogs in World War I, the Allies closed down their war dog training schools at the end of the Great War. England, France, and the United States had no official war dog training programs in place when Germany invaded Poland in 1939. Though the French Army immediately opened recruiting stations to build up their supplies of war dogs, many British strategists believed that the mechanization and modernization of warfare meant that dogs would not be as effective in World War II as they had been 20 years earlier. Therefore, when food rationing began in England and pet owners could no longer afford to feed their animals, thousands of dogs were killed there.

The British top brass weren't convinced that they needed war dogs even after reports came in that Germany had an army of 200,000 trained dogs, and were supplying Japan with dogs as well. The Germans had never stopped believing in the virtues of war dogs. Even after the Treaty of Versailles was signed at the end of World War I, Germany had continued to train war dogs. The United States reported the Germans' dog training tactics in military magazines such as *Army Ordnance* and *Infantry Journal*, but U.S. military authorities never launched their own program.

Fortunately for England, Colonel Edwin H. Richardson once again stepped in. He and another dog advocate, Major James W. Baldwin, who was in charge of an airfield in England, knew how important it was to guard equipment and supplies from enemy saboteurs. They also knew that one guard dog could do the work of six men. So, in 1939, without help from the British military authorities, Richardson and Baldwin trained several sentry dogs, and then requested that they be allowed to demonstrate what they could do. Although the demonstration was successful, and dogs began to be put to work in the war effort, it wasn't until 1942 that Britain officially set up an Army War Dog School.

In the meantime, Britain had about six hundred dogs that served unofficially with the British Expeditionary Force. The BEF and their dogs initially saw service as sentries and messengers in Poland and Belgium.

Later, in North Africa, dogs were trained to find non-metallic mines which were undetectable by standard electronic mine detectors. The dogs were taught to find soil turned over by humans planting the mines, and then to sit down several paces away. The dogs weren't very successful at this task, since sandstorms and other weather conditions

A Black Labrador

often covered up traces of freshly turned soil. No one at that time recognized that dogs could smell the chemicals in explosives.

THE BRITISH ARMY WAR DOG SCHOOL

In 1942, the British Army officially sent out a recruitment call to the public for dogs to attend war dog school. Although many pets had been killed early in the war due to food shortages, ten thousand dogs answered the first call. The Royal Society for the Prevention of Cruelty to Animals, the National Canine Defence League, and the Animal Protection Society of Scotland and Northern Ireland helped examine and register the dogs. About three and a half thousand dogs were initially accepted, including German shepherds (called Alsatians, at the time, due to anti-German sentiment), Airedales, boxers, Kerry blue terriers, working collies, bull terriers, Labradors, and curly coated retrievers. Dogs were shipped to one of several training centers located in Gloucestershire, England, and later to Burma and Egypt. By May, 1944, about seven thousand dogs had been trained for war under the command of Captain John B. Garle.

The British trained dogs to parachute out of planes, calling them "para pups." These dogs worked with the first airborne army and Special Air Service unit, and jumped from airplanes with their owners to places behind enemy lines. This idea of training dogs to jump from planes wasn't new, however.

The first known instance was in 1785 when a French balloonist named Pierre Blanchard used his pet dog for an idea he had to invent a parachute. He dropped the dog several hundred feet. Afterward, the dog ran off with the parachute and was never seen again.

The U.S. Army Air Force also experimented with parachute dogs for rescue work in the Arctic. With thousands of planes being flown from the U.S. directly to Great Britain and Russia, units of pack and rescue dogs were established in Greenland, Canada, Presque Isle and Maine. When airplanes were forced down and landing rescue vehicles was impossible due to the terrain, the Air Force tried parachuting dog teams, their sled, and a doctor directly at the crash site. They put a coat-like harness, lined with sheepskin, on the dogs. Two dogs could be placed on a 28-foot chute; one dog alone could ride on the regulation 23-foot chute.

One British dog named Rob, a black-and-white mongrel with a patch over one eye, jumped 20 times into enemy territory in North Africa and Italy. Rob was awarded the Dickin Medal, a British award for animals who displayed gallantry and devotion during World War II and afterward. The Dickin Medal was established in 1943 by Mrs. Maria Dickin, founder of the People's Royal Dispensary for Sick Animals, and is often called the animal's Victoria Cross. It was given to 53 animals – 18 dogs, 31 pigeons, three horses, and one cat – during World War II. Six of these 18 dogs received medals for bravery at home – saving victims trapped under blitzed buildings in London.

JUDY, AN ENGLISH POINTER BORN IN SHANGHAI

Other Dickin Medal recipients served far away from Mother England. Judy, a purebred English pointer, was born in Shanghai in 1936. The Royal Navy adopted her as a mascot, and she served on several gunboats. When Judy's boat was torpedoed, she was captured and sent along with her fellow sailors to a Japanese prison camp in Sumatra. Prisoners there were used to lay 3,000 miles of railway track, and conditions were terrible.

Judy attached herself to Leading Aircraftsman Frank Williams, and remained devotedly at his side even when guards began to beat him and his fellow prisoners. She distinguished herself by her hatred of the guards, who tried to shoot her several times. Judy and the prisoners were liberated in 1945. Her medal reads, "For magnificent courage and endurance in Japanese prison camps, thus helping to maintain morale among her fellow prisoners and for saving many lives by her intelligence and watchfulness."

GANDER, A CANADIAN HERO

The only Canadian dog to get the Dickin Medal was Gander, a black Newfoundland dog who was born in Newfoundland around the start of World War II. He belonged to Rod Hayden, who at that time called the dog Pal. Pal was a big dog, and although pilots landing at the nearby airport sometimes mistook him for a bear, he was much beloved by the residents of his small town.

Children used to get him to tow their sleds during winter. Unfortunately, one day Pal accidentally scratched a child's face.

Hayden, who was afraid the dog would be killed for harming the child, decided to give him to the 1st Battalion of the Royal Rifles of Canada as a mascot. The soldiers decided to rename him Gander, in honor of their base.

His handler, Fred Kelly, fed him once a day and bathed him by putting him in the shower. Kelly said Gander was playful and affectionate, and enjoyed an occasional bowl of beer.

A few months later, in 1941, the Royal Rifles and Gander were shipped out to Hong Kong to protect the British colony against the Japanese. Gander had an instinctual understanding of who the enemy was. Several times, as Japanese soldiers approached the Royal Rifles, Gander charged them and forced them to beat a retreat.

A NEWFOUNDLAND

Gander earned his medal for heroism on the night of December 19, 1941, during the battle of Lye Mun, when a Japanese grenade landed among seven Canadian soldiers. Gander picked up the grenade in his mouth and ran as fast as he could away from the men. It exploded in his mouth, killing him instantly.

Gander was awarded the Dickin Medal only recently. His story, once often told in his hometown, had almost been forgotten. But then the sister of the girl whom Gander once scratched mentioned him in a conversation with a local historian. Gander's story was revived and his handler Fred Kelly accepted his dog's medal in November, 2000.

ANTI-TANK DOGS

A less inspiring story than Gander's is that of Russia's anti-tank dogs. The Russians, who consider their dogs to be offensive weapons that are expendable, began training their dogs in 1941 to run under German tanks carrying explosives. They trained the dogs to become accustomed to carrying heavy bundles of T.N.T. strapped onto their backs. The dogs were kept hungry, and were only fed underneath running tanks. In this way, the Russians taught the dogs to eagerly anticipate the weight of the T.N.T. and the noise of approaching tanks.

Of course, once underneath a real enemy tank, the plan was to detonate the explosives – ending the Germans' and the dog's lives. But, in an almost slapstick twist, the early training backfired. Since the dogs had only been fed underneath Soviet tanks, they did not run toward the German tanks as planned. Instead, they made a beeline for Russian vehicles. This wasn't discovered until the dogs were at the Front, when an entire Russian tank division had to withdraw until their very own anti-tank dogs had been shot. Despite these mishaps, the Russians claimed that several German tanks were destroyed this way at the Battle of Kursk in 1943, and captured German papers also indicate that the anti-tank dogs were at least occasionally successful.

EVEN MORE BIZARRE

Despite early Russian mishaps with anti-tank dogs, they kept working at it, and assigned their top people to the job. Dr. Igor Valenkho at the University of Smolensk was a pioneer of Pavlovian methods for teaching tricks to mice. His goal had been to train lab mice to conduct fine repair work for use in industry and engineering, so that machines didn't have to be stripped down. But with the approach of the Wehrmacht, Valenkho was reassigned to anti-tank dog training.

His real love, however, was mice, and so he secretly continued working with them – this time training them as anti-tank mice. He knew that if he could get the mice near German tanks, they could easily get inside engines and destroy the wiring. He persuaded his superiors to drop mice from low-flying airplanes on to a German Panzer unit near Kirov in early April, 1942. This first attempt must have worked, because other drops were authorized, the most notorious being the mouse attack on 22 Panzer Division in November, 1942. One of the mice, Mikhail, was later found inside one of the disabled German tanks, proving that the mouse attack had been successful. Mikhail was given a special "Hero of the Soviet Union" medal.

But the Germans figured out what was going on after they shot down one of the Russians' mice-carrying planes. In late 1942, the Wehrmacht started adding cats to their units so that they would eat the offending mice. They had trouble keeping up with the demand for cats, however, and since there weren't enough German cats for the job, they eventually resorted to conscripting cats from other countries.

Dr. Valenkho, sorry to see his mice rendered useless, put on his thinking cap. By now, the anti-tank dog program was being given up as a failure, and dogs were being retrained for other duties. Dr. Valenkho proposed dropping several dogs with each airdrop of mice. The dogs could chase the cats, leaving the mice free to work. This brilliant idea was slightly behind the times, however, because the new Tiger tanks killed the mice with their gasoline fumes before the rodents could chew through the wires. The British then developed a plastic coating for wires which was mouse-proof, and the whole idea was, fortunately, dropped.

The U.S. tried a similar stunt. In 1943, the Army tried training dogs with timed explosives attached to their backs to attack fortified bunkers. Fortunately, problems arose immediately. Dogs sometimes turned around and headed back to their masters. Also, it was soon realized that, in actual combat, it would be very difficult to train the dogs to run to bunkers that were not occupied by Allied troops. The project, which was wisely kept secret from the public, was abandoned several months after it began. Real explosives weren't used during this training attempt, and no dogs were ever hurt.

Chapter Five

Dogs for Defense: World War II

TRAINING BEGINS

At the time of Pearl Harbor on December 7, 1941, the United States had no formal war dog training program. About 50 sled dogs were working at military stations in Alaska, where their ability to work despite snow and ice made them useful additions to mules and trucks. Another 40 dogs, who had gone on the Byrd Antarctic Expedition, were being successfully used to rescue airmen who had gone down in their planes over snowy expanses in Newfoundland, Greenland, and Iceland.

Pearl Harbor was the catalyst needed to turn attention to the potential of dogs. Just a few days after the attack, Arlene Erlanger, a nationally recognized dog breeder, called *The New York Sun* to speak to Arthur Kilbon, a reporter who had written frequently about dogs.

"I have an idea and I need your help," she said. "Our allies are training and using war dogs," she told Kilbon, and she thought the U.S.
military should follow suit. "They've got to do it," she insisted.

Together, they enlisted the help of other noted dog experts,
including Leonard Brumby, president of the Professional Handlers
Association, and Harry I. Caesar, a banker and director of the
American Kennel Club (AKC). The group established Dogs for
Defense in January, 1942, to recruit and train dogs for army use – pri-
marily as sentries along the U.S. coast and at key military installations. No one at that time considered dogs for more offensive roles.
Initially, most military officers were not even receptive to the idea of
using dogs.

But people were concerned about the growing risk of saboteurs and
enemy aliens damaging civilian war plants and military installations.
Lt. Col. Clifford C. Smith, who was in charge of plant protection for the
Army's Quartermaster Corps, proposed to his commanding general that
sentry dogs be used to support army supply depot guards. Major
General Edmund B. Gregory approved an experimental program, and
requested 200 sentry dogs in March, 1942. The first official U.S. war
dog training program had begun.

The decision to begin training dogs for sentry duty was validated
just three months later. In June, four German spies ran aground in their
submarine off the coast of Long Island. John Cullen, a coast guardsman
based in Amagansett, New York, was making his six-mile patrol on the
beach at around midnight when he encountered the men. Fortunately,
they let him walk off without harm, but Cullen immediately reported it
to his superiors. The next day, the Coast Guard found explosives hidden
in the dunes.

With the help of the FBI, the four agents, plus four German men who had landed in Florida, were captured. Germany had armed them with money and explosives and told them to bomb factories and railroads.

This made the Coast Guard recognize how vulnerable U.S. shorelines were, so they quickly enlisted more help. In August of 1942, the Coast Guard began the first beach patrols using dogs – and, by the end of the war, over nine thousand dogs had stood sentry at U.S. installations and along the coastline.

The Army's war dog training program was experimental for many different reasons – most obviously, because the majority of U.S. military personnel had never used dogs and needed to be convinced that they could be an asset. It was also experimental because neither the military nor any civilian had ever run a program like it before. Everything was new – supplying the dogs, training them, sheltering them, and training soldiers to use the dogs. Dogs for Defense enlisted the cooperation of the American Kennel Club, which, as the registration body for all purebred dogs, had a strong influence upon owners. The AKC also helped finance the operation of Dogs for Defense.

To fill the Quartermaster's order for two hundred dogs to be trained as sentries, Dogs for Defense called upon 402 kennel clubs across the country for the donation of dogs. Civilians – even famous ones – were eager to help too. Greer Garson sent her poodle, Cliquot; Mary Pickford gave her German shepherd, Silver; Rudy Valee gave his Doberman pinscher, King. Metropolitan Opera star Ezio Pinza sent his two Dalmatians, Boris and Figaro, with one of his albums to the training center with the dogs. "If they get lonesome," he said, "play one of these records for them!" Owners surrendered their dogs to Dogs for Defense unconditionally.

Only once was a dog returned home at the request of his owner. Just ten hours after this particular dog was dropped off, the owner called and said that the pet's absence had caused his wife to collapse. The dog was promptly returned home.

A Few Rough Edges

As with many new programs, things did not go smoothly at first, despite everyone's best intentions. Since no single kennel was large enough to train 200 dogs, they were shipped to a dozen private kennels. Qualified trainers volunteered their services without pay. The lack of a single place in which to train dogs, and the multitude of trainers, each with his or her own technique, meant that at first the dogs made little progress. Most instructors had no experience of teaching sentry dogs and were unfamiliar with military conditions. Equally important to the lack of initial success was the fact that the Army didn't make enlisted men available for training as dog handlers. Because no soldiers were learning how to work with them, the dogs were useless in the field.

Despite these setbacks, interest in war dogs was expanding. In July 1942, the Secretary of War told the Quartermaster General to broaden the war dog training program beyond sentry duty to include preparing dogs for scout, messenger, and sled work. The Quartermaster General was also ordered to teach handlers, develop training techniques, and establish schools which could be rapidly expanded. Thus, six months after the establishment of the civilian-run Dogs for Defense, the military had fully embraced the idea of training dogs in large numbers for a wide variety of tactical purposes and wartime services. By December, the Quartermaster General announced that the U.S. military was seeking 125,000 dogs. Although this number was later reduced, the war dog training effort was now steaming ahead.

A SIBERIAN HUSKY

To accomplish these more ambitious goals, the Army decided to take over responsibility for training the animals. The Army's Remount Branch of the Quartermaster Corps (QMC) was well equipped to handle dog training based on its history of dealing with horses and mules. Dogs for Defense retained control of finding dogs, which they then sent to QMC-managed reception centers. A strong regional presence, enthusiastic volunteers, and good publicity made Dogs for Defense successful in obtaining dogs throughout the war effort. About 40 percent of the animals passed the preliminary physical exam required before being sent to the training centers.

There, the dogs were examined by veterinarians, classified as to their suitability for particular roles, and then trained. Experience had taught the army that dog handlers were as important as their dogs, so they were taught alongside their dogs to work as a unit. Dog and man traveled as a team to their training center, and the policy was to keep dog and handler together throughout their military careers. Only the handler was allowed to feed, pet, or make the dog work for fear that otherwise he would become more a mascot than a soldier. By this time, the war dog program was being called the K-9 Corps, in reference to the word "canine." *The New York Times* tried to adopt the name WAAGS for the dogs, but fortunately few others followed suit.

LESSONS LEARNED

Over the course of World War II, about 20,000 dogs were procured and sent for training. Only half actually graduated. The others were disqualified due to disease, unsuitable temperament, inferior scenting powers, and excitability around noise or gunfire. As time went on, the military got smarter about which dogs were best suited to which types of work. In the beginning, when most dogs were being trained as sentries, more than 30 breeds were accepted. Soon it became apparent that Great Danes, which were too large, and hunting breeds, which were easily distracted by animal scents, were not gifted war dogs. By 1944, the seven breeds, and their cross-breeds, considered to be the best for training as "dog soldiers" were German shepherds, Belgian sheep dogs, Doberman pinschers, farm collies, Siberian huskies, Malamutes and Eskimo dogs.

Young dogs, between one to two years old, were preferred because they were easier to train.

The first month of the two- to three-month course was devoted to teaching the animals certain basic patterns of behavior necessary for all war dogs to exhibit. The dogs learned to obey verbal commands and gestures, and were exposed to muzzles, gas masks, riding in cars and trucks, and gunfire. Their handlers learned about grooming, feeding, and the capabilities and limitations of dogs. By the second month, the dog had been assigned to a particular type of training based upon his temperament and aptitude. A dog might be trained for one of five different roles. They were: sentry, scout, messenger, sled and pack-bearer, and mine detector.

Over the course of the war, the Army learned a lot about how dogs could best be used. Eventually, it was concluded that sentry dogs and scout dogs were most useful. Pack and sled dogs were ultimately replaced by helicopters. The training of mine detection dogs was stopped after tests in North Africa showed that dogs could find only about half the mines. Feelings were mixed about the use of messenger dogs. Some people reported excellent results, but their use was limited to certain conditions.

Sentry Dogs

More than 9,000 of the 10,425 dogs trained at the war dog centers during World War II were prepared for sentry duty, and most of those dogs served at home in the United States, guarding the coastline and military installations. By 1943, the threat to U.S. shorelines and war plants had markedly decreased, and the need for new sentry dogs slowed down, while the demand for scout dogs was steadily increasing. Soon, sentry dogs were being returned to the training centers faster than they were being shipped out. Nonetheless, there are many stories of dog sentries saving the day.

THE BOXER ROLF

In addition to learning how to detect an intruder, sentry dogs were sometimes trained to attack the enemy as well. An attack dog had to be naturally aggressive, and big enough to overpower a man. He was taught to attack only upon command.

One such dog was Rolf, a boxer, who was stationed as a sentry at a war plant in Boston. One night, Rolf alerted his handler, who told him to attack a burglar. Rolf grabbed onto the intruder with his teeth, and, despite a skirmish, didn't let go until his handler had captured the man, who happened to be holding plans for the demolition of the factory.

CHIPS, THE MIXED BREED HERO

The first, and probably the most famous, sentry dog hero was Chips. Chips was a mixed breed, whose father was part German shepherd, part collie, and whose mother was a sled dog. He was donated to the war effort by Edward J. Wren of Pleasantville, New York, and completed sentry training in early 1942 in Virginia.

He was assigned to Private John P. Rowell of the 30th Infantry, 3rd Infantry Division, and, in October, both were shipped out to French Morocco as part of the North African invasion. Mena, one of the three other dogs in the detachment on board, apparently took a liking to Chips, for some time later she gave birth to nine of Chips' pups.

When Chips and his unit landed on the Vichy-held beaches of Fedallah, shore batteries opened fire. Mena began to cower, and ultimately was returned to the United States because of her fears.

A BOXER

But Chips remained unfazed throughout his tour of duty. He and the other sentry dogs provided perimeter defense, and it was reported that no one died when dogs were posted as sentries.

The 3rd Infantry Division soon received orders to guard the Roosevelt–Churchill conference between January 14 and January 23, 1943. Chips and three other sentry dogs were chosen with their handlers to provide guard service for it – a great honor.

On July 10, Chips arrived with the 3rd Division in Sicily, as part of Brigadier General George S. Patton's 7th Army. Chips and the soldiers made their way ashore and established a beachhead.

Early in the morning, at 4:20 a.m., Chips and Rowell were working toward what looked like a small, grass-covered hut. It appeared to be a good place to bivouac for a much-needed rest. But suddenly, the silence was broken by the rat-a-tat-tat of machine gun fire. Chips wrenched his leash from Rowell's hand, and began running toward the hut, which was actually a camouflaged pillbox. He dashed into the machine gun nest, and the firing stopped.

All was quiet for a moment, until an Italian soldier came out of the hut with Chips snarling and biting him. Three other soldiers walked out of the hut with their arms raised. Rowell called Chips off and took the Italians prisoner.

Chips, who had powder burns and a minor scalp wound, inflicted when the Italians tried to shoot him with a revolver, was treated by medics and released to Rowell that evening. Later that night, he alerted his handler to ten more Italian enemies, whom Rowell also took prisoner.

Chips soon became widely known throughout the 3rd Division, and the press made hay with the story. Everyone loved hearing about the hero dog, and two congressmen even made speeches about him in Washington. In October, 1943, Chips received a citation for a Silver Star and a Purple Heart, despite the regulation prohibiting animals from receiving medals. By this time, Chips was in Italy, participating in the Naples–Foggia and the Rome–Arno campaigns. General Eisenhower met the dog and tried to pet him, but Chips nipped his hand. He was clearly tiring from the constant stress of battle, and soon afterward was transferred away from the Front lines to the rear for sentry duty.

In the meantime, the national commander of the Military Order of the Purple Heart had caught wind of Chips' Purple Heart and Silver Star. He didn't like the idea that dogs could receive the same medal as soldiers, and said so in a letter to President Roosevelt. He demanded that Chips' medals be removed, which they later were. To his credit, the commander did suggest that a special medal be created for animals, the way the Dickin Medal was created in Great Britain, but this was never done.

Chips was sent back to his training center in Virginia at the end of the war in October, 1945. The Wren family wanted Chips back, and so, in December of 1945, he traveled by train with six reporters and photographers to his home in Pleasantville. He died there several months later. The men of his unit couldn't let Chips go undecorated—they unofficially awarded him the Theater Ribbon with the arrowhead for an assault landing and a Battle Star for each of the eight campaigns in which he participated.

SCOUT DOGS

Chips' heroism paved the way for the military to think more seriously about using dogs for more than just guard duty. By 1943, the Army's Quartermaster Corps had already begun training scout and messenger dogs.

The training was limited to a few dogs, because most officers were skeptical about the use of dogs in combat. Many believed that dogs weren't suited to the tropics. And there had been reports from the British that their scout and messenger dogs had not performed well in North Africa, although it was suggested that dogs might be better suited to the dense underbrush of the Pacific.

Efforts to train tactical dogs were also hampered, at first, by a lack of trainers experienced in scout and messenger work. So England's Director of the War Dog Training School, Captain John Garle, together with two handlers and four dogs, agreed to come to the U.S. to teach his dog training techniques. He was so impressive that the Army asked him to travel to all the training centers to indoctrinate trainers in his methods.

Scout dogs were trained to give silent warning of the approach of any enemy. Unlike sentry dogs, which generally worked on the leash, scout dogs could work both on and off the leash. A scout dog could range up to 75 feet from his handler, making it possible to send the dog ahead on trails and to investigate apparently abandoned buildings. Although the distance at which dogs could detect the enemy depended on wind, humidity, and terrain, they could always sense danger sooner than men because of their acute senses of smell and hearing. Training focused on stimulating a dogs' senses – he was taught to detect human scent as a bird dog is trained to detect hidden birds. When a scout dog smelled the enemy, he communicated with his handler by stiffening his body, raising his hackles, pricking his ears, and holding his tail rigid. Such dogs were taught to be silent at all times, and were exposed early in their training to heavy gunfire so they would learn not to be afraid.

Scout dogs were assigned mostly to reconnaissance and combat patrols at outposts. While on patrol, a dog and his handler usually traveled a short distance in front of the patrol, moving so that the wind and other conditions favored the dog's power of scenting. If the dog scented the enemy, the handler signaled the patrol leader, who then gave commands. At outposts, the scout dog and his master would position themselves a short distance from the unit, and the dog would remain alert while stationary.

PEEFKE, THE GERMAN SHEPHERD SCOUT

Peefke was a scout dog working with the Army in the Italian Alps. Though he was a strong German shepherd, leading patrol troops through the heavy snow was hard work. One day, on a seemingly empty trail, Peefke stopped. His handler saw that Peefke had become alert and stationary, but he saw no sign of the enemy. The handler then looked again, more carefully. This time, he saw a trip wire, stretched nearly invisibly across the trail. The wire was attached to three enemy "S" mines, which would have killed the entire patrol. Peefke saved countless other lives throughout his tour of duty, which ended in 1945 when he was killed by a hand grenade.

MESSENGER DOGS

Messenger dogs were often used with scout dogs and delivered communications from a scouting patrol to headquarters. Strong loyalty was the most important qualification for messenger dogs, because their attachment to their masters determined to what lengths they would go to get a communication through enemy lines. A messenger dog needed two handlers to whom he was loyal, since he had to run between two points. Dual loyalty was taught by having each handler take turns at teaching and feeding the animal. During training, the two handlers would hide as much as a mile away from the dog so the animal could learn to locate them by body scent.

In the spring of 1943, to test the usefulness of scout and messenger dogs, the War Department decided to send a detachment of six scout and two messenger dogs overseas to Army troops in the Pacific. In New Guinea, and later in New Britain, the dogs proved themselves to be a great asset. In December, in New Britain, the eight dogs went on 48 patrols in 53 days. No men were killed in patrols with dogs in attendance. Units without dogs, however, did suffer casualties. The Army officially credited the patrols that used scout dogs with killing 180 and capturing 20 Japanese soldiers.

SANDY, THE GERMAN SHEPHERD MESSENGER

A German shepherd named Sandy, one of the dogs in this early experimental detatchment, distinguished himself from the start by being unafraid of battle noise. He quickly became the best messenger of his war dog group and became a hero in the campaign near Turzi Point in New Britain.

Japanese snipers in pillboxes were holding up U.S. Marines who were advancing towards an air-strip. The U.S. needed reinforcements in order to get through Japanese defenses, but heavy rains had made their walkie-talkies useless, so they couldn't reach headquarters for help. Sandy's handler, Sergeant Brown, put a message in a pouch tied around Sandy's neck and sent him to his other handler, Sergeant Sheldon. Unbeknownst to Sandy, Sheldon had moved the night before to a new location near the battalion command post.

Sandy took off under heavy gunfire. He swam a river, jumped barbed wire, and eventually found Sheldon, who was in a foxhole. Sandy jumped into the foxhole, right on top of Sheldon.

"I didn't even know Sandy was coming until he landed on me, panting and dripping," Sheldon later said.

After reading the message, the battalion commander directed heavy artillery toward the Japanese pillboxes. The Marines prevailed, and Sandy was a hero.

THE FIRST WAR DOG PLATOONS

The success of this first experimental detachment in the Pacific led the War Department to officially establish war dog platoons in March, 1944. Originally, an army dog platoon consisted of 12 scout dogs, 12 messenger dogs, one mine detection dog, and 27 men. Three months later, however, after much trial and error, the balance changed so that a platoon had 18 scout dogs, six messenger dogs, and 20 men. The mine detection dog was eliminated. By year's end, messenger dogs had been eliminated too. Electronic communication was becoming so reliable that messenger dogs weren't necessary.

The scout dog emerged as far and away the most valuable dog, and, by the end of 1944, war dog platoons consisted of 27 scout dogs. When the war ended, 436 scout dogs had been trained and sent overseas, and demand was still increasing.

Meanwhile, the Marines had also embarked on training scout and messenger dogs. After heavy losses due to ambushes in the dense jungles on Guadalcanal in August, 1942, the commandant of the Marine Corps requested a dog training program. The Marine dogs became known as the Devildogs, based on the German nickname for the tenacious Marines during World War I. The first group of dogs, all Dobermans, started training at Camp Lejeune in January, 1943. They became the 1st Marine War Dog Platoon and were shipped out to the Pacific in June that same year.

The eight war dog platoons that served in the Pacific during the course of the war were more effective than the seven dog platoons that served in the European theater. In Europe, deep snow, open spaces, and static fronts didn't allow the dogs to utilize their powerful abilities for early detection of the enemy. In the Pacific, dogs were able to navigate the dense tropical vegetation and the semi-darkness of the jungles better than people could. Dogs also worked well in heavily wooded terrain, on mountains, and along river bottoms.

Dog platoons also greatly reduced the danger of ambush and boosted the morale of soldiers. When a dog was on patrol, everyone relaxed a little. This enabled the patrols to operate more efficiently and to cover greater distances.

The 1st Marine War Dog Platoon counted many acts of heroism from the dogs in its ranks. The dogs' first assignment took them to Bougainville in the Solomon Islands. It was November, 1943. Right from the start, the platoon was successful, and proved how useful dogs could be in the dense Pacific jungles. General Thomas Holcomb, commandant of the Marine Corps, was so impressed with the war dogs that he wrote several letters home to the original owners of the dogs, describing their bravery.

Andy – A Scout Dog

The Japanese on Bougainville were well fortified, and the Marines who assaulted the beach had to deal with heavy gunfire. Within hours of

A BLACK AND TAN DOBERMAN

landing, the dogs of the 1st Marine War Dog Platoon were put to work.

A big black Doberman named Andy, and his two handlers, Pfc. Robert Lansley and Pfc. John Mahoney, were sent to the M Company, a 250-man patrol, to lead the company inland. Their objective was to reach the junction of two trails, and to block off the Japanese from bringing in reinforcements.

The Piva Trail hardly seemed like a trail at all. It was covered with dense jungle which offered easy cover for the enemy. Andy worked off-leash about 25 yards in front of the men – one of the few dogs present capable of working off-leash. If he sensed something amiss, Andy would freeze, and the hair on his neck and back would stand straight up. If the dog moved too far ahead, Lansley would cluck to bring him back.

As they moved forward, Andy alerted many times to Japanese sniper positions. One time after Andy alerted, Lansley and Mahoney dropped quickly, and missed being hit by machine gun fire by only two feet.

Two other times, Andy alerted so that the Marines were able to surround and eliminate the enemy patrols. As a result, the M Company cut off the Japanese at the head of the trail, and also gained the most territory of any platoon that first day of the invasion.

On the fourteenth day of the 1st Marine War Dog Platoon's presence in Bougainville, Andy proved himself again. The Marines had been stopped in their advance by machine gun fire. But no one knew where it was coming from. Lansley and Mahoney volunteered to scout out the enemy position with Andy. The three set off into the jungle. Andy froze, but this time his signals were all mixed up. He pointed left, and then he pointed right. With Mahoney covering him, Lansley crawled up beside Andy. Through the underbrush, he saw a small trail, straddled on either side by two large Banyan trees. The trees were common to

Bougainville, but something about them seemed unusual. Lansley noticed that the bushes covering the roots looked strange, and he guessed that they were covering machine gun nests set up on either side of the trail to create cross-fire. Lansley sprayed machine gun fire into the nests, and then threw grenades in them. Again, a potential disaster had been avoided, and Andy was a hero.

Holcomb wrote to Andy's owner back in the United States, Theodore Widermann of Norristown, Pennsylvania, with the following report: "Andy...gave warning of scattered Japanese sniper opposition on many occasions, and was undoubtedly the means of preventing the loss of life of Marines."

CAESAR, THE GERMAN SHEPHERD SENTRY AND MESSENGER

Another dog with M Company was Caesar, a three-year-old German shepherd who had been donated by the Glazer family of Philadelphia. The family already had all three of their sons in the war, so donating their dog to the war effort wasn't easy for them.

Caesar was trained as a sentry and messenger dog, and very early on distinguished himself as being particularly intelligent. The handlers assigned to Caesar, Rufus Mayo and John Kleeman, adored Caesar, and said so in several letters they both wrote home to their families. Mayo liked and respected Caesar so much that he had the dog plant his paw print on every letter the soldier sent home.

Caesar, Mayo, and Kleeman landed with the 1st Marine War Dog Platoon on Bougainville on D day, November 1. The first 11 days on Bougainville were a harsh introduction to the realities of tropical weather – a downpour continued nonstop for most of that time. The heavy rains took out most of the walkie talkies, and the ones that did work had limited range due to the dense jungle underbrush. Telephone wire had not yet been laid, so communication was extremely difficult.

For the first 48 hours of the invasion, Caesar was the only means of communication between the front lines and the battalion command post. He completed nine missions altogether, two of them under heavy fire, running between his two handlers until he was exhausted.

On the second night, the commanding officer asked Mayo and Caesar to sleep in a foxhole several hundred yards in front of the rest of the company, to act as sentries. The Japanese had been very successful at infiltrating American outposts under cover of night, and it was Mayo's and Caesar's job to warn their unit of danger.

Early the next morning, Mayo woke up when Caesar suddenly jumped out of the foxhole. Mayo called him back, but just as Caesar was turning to obey, a Japanese sniper began firing. In the firefight, the dog was shot twice, and he disappeared into the underbrush. Mayo was frantic.

He and some other soldiers followed a trail of blood which led back to the command post, where they found Caesar lying in some bushes. He had tried to drag himself back to Kleeman, his second handler.

The men rigged up a stretcher out of an old blanket. A dozen Marines volunteered to bear Caesar to the first aid station. Many others saluted the dog as he was carried by. Outside the hospital tent, Mayo anxiously awaited news of the dog's condition. The doctor removed one bullet, but left the other in because it was so close to the dog's heart.

Caesar returned to active duty in three weeks.

JACK, THE BELGIAN SHEPHERD MESSENGER

Jack was a messenger dog who was so loyal to his handlers that he went on a critical mission even after he had already been wounded. Jack, a

A BELGIAN SHEPHERD

Belgian shepherd, did not have promising beginnings – he had been left at an animal shelter in Long Island by someone recently drafted into the Army. He was taken home by Joseph Varhaeghe, who went to the shelter to find a dog for his son Bobby. Varhaeghe tried to enlist in the Army himself, but was turned down. Instead, he and Bobby agreed they should send Jack.

Jack was assigned to the 1st Marine War Dog Platoon. He and his two handlers, Gordon Wortman and Paul Castracane, were part of a unit that moved far inland on Bougainville, and manned a roadblock.

On the seventh day of the invasion, Japanese troops attacked the roadblock, and cut telephone lines. Things for the Marines were not looking good. Wortman was hit in the leg, and Jack took a bullet in the back. Reinforcements and first aid were essential for them if they were to avoid losing the skirmish.

The commanding officer crawled over to Wortman, and asked his permission to send the wounded dog to headquarters. Wortman put a message in the pouch around Jack's back and commanded him to report to Castracane, who was back at headquarters. Everyone watched as Jack struggled to stand, and then took off amid a hail of bullets.

Jack made it to Castracane, and then collapsed at his feet, blood pouring from his wounds. Headquarters sent help, and many lives were saved that day in addition to Wortman's – thanks to Jack's loyalty.

ROLO THE SCOUT

Rolo was one of only two dogs to die on Bougainville. He was a scout dog who had already seen two months of active patrol duty there with the 1st Marine War Dog Platoon. Rolo and his two handlers, Russell

A DOBERMAN PINSCHER

Friedrich and James White, had been temporarily assigned to an army unit. Their mission was to find Japanese hiding along the Torokina river.

The patrol was about 3,000 yards into the jungle, with Friedrich and Rolo in the lead, when Rolo alerted. Friedrich notified the army patrol leader, but the officer didn't believe Rolo, and ordered the men forward. They walked right into a Japanese ambush. Amid the hail of bullets, Friedrich decided Rolo would be safer with White, and sent him off. But when Rolo reached his other handler, the bullets started coming closer to White, who sent Rolo back to Friedrich. Just as he reached Friedrich, Rolo got hit, and then died. Friedrich also got hit, and at that point his army patrol withdrew. Later, the Marines went back to search for Friedrich, but found only Rolo. Friedrich was listed as missing in action.

CARL, THE DOBERMAN PINSCHER SENTRY

The Marine's 1st War Dog Platoon was such a success that others soon followed. Beginning in 1944, army and marine war dog platoons went on thousands of patrols throughout the Pacific. Much of the campaign there consisted of island hopping, and once again dogs proved their worth.

Carl was a sentry dog, a Doberman pinscher who landed in Iwo Jima in the South Pacific in February, 1945, with the Marines of the 28th regiment. He and his handler, Pfc. Raymond Moquin, were on security watch one night in a foxhole. Their foxhole was well ahead of the rest of the troops so they could alert them of danger. But their position meant that it was difficult to communicate. Before night fell, Moquin rigged up a string from his foxhole and tied it to the hands of marines in the nearest foxholes. A tug on the string would be a warning signal.

By the middle of the night, most of the Marines were getting some much needed sleep. But Carl began to sense danger, and he alerted many times – signifying the presence of many enemy soldiers. Moquin pulled on the string, waking the Marines.

By the time the Japanese attacked 30 minutes later, the Marines were well prepared. Over 100 Japanese soldiers lost their lives in that battle, but only two Americans were hurt.

RETURN TO CIVILIAN LIFE

By the close of World War II, it was generally agreed that the war dogs had performed admirably and saved thousands of lives. The dogs were recognized officially with honors certificates. Dogs killed in action were given Certificates of Merit, and dogs retired from service were given a Discharge Certificate. Medals were not officially allowed after the disaster with Chips, but dogs could be commended in general and unit orders. Much had been learned about the conditions under which dogs performed best, and about the inherent strengths and limitations of dogs. The program's success was indicated by the Army's intention to establish a total of sixty-five scout dog platoons. When the war ended, this ambitious plan was replaced by another one – the plan to return thousands of war dogs to civilian life.

This was not an easy task to accomplish. There were many hurdles: detraining the dogs, shipping, feeding, and caring for them until they found new homes, and finding new owners for them. Detraining took eight to 12 weeks, and began by having the dogs handled by several people so that they would learn not to be suspicious of strangers. Eventually, dogs were confronted by aggressive people in various situations, and taught to be conciliatory rather than to attack. Only a few dogs could not be detrained and had to be destroyed. In all, 3,000 dogs were returned to civilian life. Only four needed to be returned to the military.

Finding new homes for the dogs was not a problem. Original owners who requested their dogs back received not only the dog, but also a certificate of faithful service, a collar, a leash, and an army manual entitled *War Dogs*. All the dogs recognized their masters and were happy to see them. In fact, the public demand for dogs with no original owners was much greater than the supply and requests poured in long after all the dogs were given away.

Chapter Six

Vietnam Begins

CULTURAL DIFFERENCES

In 1954, when South and North Vietnam were split apart, President Dwight D. Eisenhower sent civilian advisors to South Vietnam. Relatively small numbers of these "advisors," who dressed in U.S. military uniforms, continued working in Vietnam until 1961. That year, President John F. Kennedy sent ten thousand Americans to Vietnam, in what was the start of a slow and steady build-up of Americans.

Remembering lessons learned in World War II, the U.S. military recognized that dogs could be helpful in South Vietnam's war against communist Vietcong (VC) guerillas. So, in 1961, the Americans' Military Assistance Advisory Group, Vietnam (MAAGV) recommended that the South Vietnamese army, called the Army of the Republic of Vietnam (ARVN), use military dogs for sentry and scout work.

The Department of Defense authorized 300 dogs to start the ARVN program. Dogs were bought and trained in West Germany, at a dog training center there under the command of Captain Barton H. Patterson and veterinarian Captain William E. Callahan. The two men scoured the West German countryside looking for suitable German shepherds, and purchased the dogs for $40 each. The dogs were shipped to South Vietnam in the middle of 1962, where they were met by ARVN soldiers who were to begin training as handlers and veterinary assistants.

The first meeting between the newly-arrived dogs from West Germany and the Vietnamese trainees was an omen of things to come. The dogs were initially frightened by the Vietnamese and kept breaking away from them and running back to their American handlers. According to one witness, the dogs weren't used to Asians, and couldn't understand the Vietnamese pronunciation of their names. Ultimately, however, the dogs gave their complete loyalty to their new masters, and became afraid of Caucasians.

But the program was ill-fated from the start, due in large part to insurmountable cultural differences between the way the Vietnamese and the Americans viewed dogs. An American trainer named Jesse Mendez, who was sent to work with the ARVN dog handlers, said that one problem was that many Vietnamese were Buddhists who believed in reincarnation. Mendez speculated that, by working with the dogs, the ARVN soldiers feared that they would be reincarnated as dogs. Another issue was the South Vietnamese soldiers' refusal to praise their dogs, which was necessary to effectively train and reward the canines. Since some of the German shepherds weighed in at eighty pounds or more, the small Vietnamese soldiers, who sometimes weighed only ten to 15 pounds more than the dogs, may have been physically intimidated by them.

In addition, there was a serious lack of medical care provided for the dogs. There were only about 20 veterinarians in all of South Vietnam, and most of them were too old to practice medicine at all. Only four of the 20 worked for the ARVN and none of them had ever worked with dogs. A vet in Vietnam would have no need of experience with dogs, because no Vietnamese person would have thought of paying to have a dog medically treated. Most people there were unable to afford their own healthcare, much less that of a pet.

Food, or the lack of it, was another problem for the dogs. The diet recommended by the Americans to keep the dogs in top physical condition was great, in theory. But, in practice, to follow it, the ARVN would have had to spend more money feeding a dog every day than on a soldier's daily rations. Over the next few years, 90 percent of ARVN dog deaths were due to malnutrition. Moreover, many Vietnamese ate dogs. They were not the treasured pets that they are in the United States.

The result was a high dog mortality rate in Vietnam. In addition to malnutrition, dogs also died from disease and accidents. Spoiled food, heat stroke and dehydration, and snakebites were other common killers. Very few dogs were killed on duty. Although by 1964 there were 327 dogs being used by the South Vietnamese army, the program never grew to its target size of 1,000 dogs. By 1966, the ARVN dog population had dropped to 130 scouts and sentries.

SUZI

Not all dogs were given by Americans to the Vietnamese. One enterprising Green Beret adopted a Vietnamese dog that saved his life. Paul Morgan, a 19-year-old from the Bronx, enlisted in the Army in 1957 with the 82nd Airborne Division. He also trained as a dog handler, although he was never assigned to a dog platoon. But he knew how valuable a dog could be, and he quickly made use of that knowledge when he arrived in Vietnam in June, 1965. He was assigned to the 30th Ranger Battalion, and stationed in Cau Xang, a small village in the rice paddies and pineapple fields 30 miles west of Saigon.

The village was a Catholic community with a very active priest, Father Nguyen Cong Tu. Father Tu was a strong anti-communist who had served several years in jail after Vietnam was divided. South Vietnam's Vietcong guerillas hated Father Tu and had placed a bounty on him, for he was both a spiritual leader and a guerilla fighter.

Father Tu had a German shepherd named Xa Xi after the Vietnamese word for sarsaparilla, a soda which the dog loved to drink. Xa Xi had guarded Father Tu for several years, viciously attacking anyone who threatened her owner.

Morgan, a Catholic who went to mass every day, became friendly with Father Tu. One day, Morgan presented Father Tu with a .38 caliber pistol and a set of sterling silver rosary beads, which were too delicate for a soldier's life in Vietnam.

In return for Morgan's kind gift, Father Tu gave Morgan his dog, who soon became known as Suzi. Father Tu told Morgan that God protects dogs from the knowledge of death so that they can stand by their master in all difficulties. Suzi slept next to Morgan every night, tied to his wrist with parachute cord. She was obedient, faithful, and devoted, and was always by the young soldier's side.

On September 29, three months after Morgan had arrived in Vietnam, he got his first real taste of combat. Morgan was just outside Saigon, preparing to take a convoy of supplies of ammunition back to his battalion's home base at Cau Xang. Morgan was with a company of 12 Vietnamese (ARVN) Rangers on detail that day, led by Sergeant Nhan. The Rangers reported for duty one-by-one early in the morning. Morgan and the others sat drinking coffee and smoking Vietnamese cigarettes, called Ruby Queens. One of the last troopers to arrive tumbled out of a taxi, his red eyes indicating the ill effects of the night before. He was strong and big, and Suzi instantly began growling at him.

The convoy moved out on the road to Cau Xang. As they traveled through one village after another, the tension began to mount. The ammunition they carried was coveted by the Vietcong, who were probably watching their every move. Morgan knew that they must continue moving because a stationary convoy was an easy target.

They were on an open road about 15 miles outside Saigon, when shots were fired at the rear of the convoy. "An ambush," Morgan thought. They picked up speed, and began racing down the road. There were no villages in sight, only water buffalo in the rice paddies. The boys who usually tended the beasts, and whom the American soldiers called Buffalo Bills, were hiding. The convoy raced the next five miles to Cau Xang with shots ringing out constantly at the rear, but, miraculously, they weren't hit.

When they arrived at Cau Xang, Captain Nguyen Chi Tot, the ranger battalion commander, was unaccountably furious. He screamed at Sergeant Nhan and at Morgan, despite the fact that Suzi was guarding her master ferociously. Next, the Captain lined up the 12 AVRN Rangers, and suddenly attacked one soldier with a bamboo walking stick. It was the soldier with the red eyes, and he was beaten to the ground, disarmed, and kicked brutally. Morgan couldn't believe how cruelly Red Eyes was being treated.

But Captain Tot knew some things that Sergeant Nahn and Morgan did not know. It turned out that Red Eyes had been the one firing from the back of the convoy. He had been aiming at the water buffalo, but the battalion commander suspected that he was also alerting the Vietcong to the convoy's position. Red Eyes had deserted the unit several months earlier and had returned to the battalion without authorization. Giving him a ranger uniform and a machine gun had been a mistake, he felt. Captain Tot was sure that Red Eyes had become a traitor, and was now working with the Vietcong.

Subsequently, Red Eyes was put into a tiger cage which was three feet high, three feet wide, and three feet deep. It was too short to stand in and too small to lie down in. The cage was put in the sun, with no protection. The prisoner was stripped to his shorts, bound hand and foot, and not given any food or water. Morgan couldn't stand the inhumanity of Red Eyes' treatment, but he was powerless to intervene.

That night, Red Eyes was let out of the tiger cage to eat. He overpowered the guards, grabbed a hand grenade, and ran to battalion headquarters, where Captain Tot, Morgan, and some others were eating. Red Eyes pulled the pin on the grenade, and told everyone they were about to die. But before he knew it, three other AVRN Rangers wrestled him down, and put the pin back in the grenade to deactivate it. Red Eyes was taken back to the tiger cage and would be taken to prison in Saigon the next day, said Captain Tot, who remained calm throughout the episode and afterward smoked a cigar. But Morgan was rattled, and couldn't relax.

At about 10 o'clock that night, a large Vietcong battalion attacked the village. This was the first time Morgan had seen the enemy out in the open. Enemy mortar fire was hitting the village, and it began to catch fire. Civilians and soldiers alike needed medical treatment. The scene was chaotic.

Suddenly, the mortars went silent. Without the mortars, which lit up the night sky with parachute flares, the helicopter gunships couldn't fire on the Vietcong. The enemy was beginning to infiltrate the village, and, without fire support from the artillery and the gunships, it was likely that the Vietcong would overrun the village. Morgan was ordered to get the mortars running again.

With Suzi at his side, Morgan began creeping through the dark village, trying to find the mortar pit. Along the way, Sergeant Nahn joined Morgan, then Corporal Phung. After what seemed like an eternity, they finally found the pit. There, they found one crew member dead, blown up by a grenade, and three others seriously wounded. Morgan, Nahn, and Phung quickly moved the men out of the pit so they could fire the mortars. Morgan dropped two illuminating flares down the tube, and radioed to headquarters that they were about to shoot them off.

Just then, Suzi alerted, and then she began to bark viciously. Nahn looked up, and yelled, "Look out!" Morgan wheeled around, and saw a man wearing a U.S. ranger uniform about to throw a grenade at them. Nahn fired his M-14 at the man, and Morgan hit him with a .45 pistol.

The man went down, and Phung jumped on the grenade, which exploded, killing him. Nahn was wounded in the arm by grenade fragments, but Suzi and Morgan were unharmed.

The man turned out to be Red Eyes. His head had been blown off, but, even in death, he looked mean and crazed, just as he had early that same morning. Apparently, someone had let him out of the tiger cage when he had been wounded when the fighting had begun. He had killed two rangers, and taken their clothes and equipment. Then he had attacked the men in the mortar position with grenades. Captain Tot's worst fears were realised – Red Eyes was a traitor.

Thanks to Suzi, the mortars began firing again, illuminating the night so that helicopter gunships could support the ground units. The Vietcong withdrew.

Suzi's alert had enabled Morgan and Nahn to silence Red Eyes, and Phung's heroism had saved their lives. Morgan received an Army Commendation Medal for this baptism of fire, but, to his regret, Suzi received no mention.

U.S. WAR DOGS REACTIVATED

In the years between 1961 and 1965, the American presence in Vietnam built up bit by bit, and American "advisors" were killed by ones and twos. But in 1964, the North Vietnamese Communists decided they needed to help the Vietcong guerillas in South Vietnam. They planned a campaign for October, 1965, which would crush the ARVN and the American Special Forces Camp at Plei Me – with the ultimate goal of "liberating" all of South Vietnam. Meanwhile, terrorist attacks on U.S. strongholds grew more frequent. In February, 1965, Vietcong guerillas mortared and mined the U.S. airbase in Pleiku, where eight Americans were killed and over 100 wounded. In the months that followed, President Lyndon B. Johnson authorized thousands more troops to be sent to Vietnam.

A BLACK AND TAN GERMAN SHEPHERD.

Casualties were no longer occuring in pairs – they were coming in by the bucket load. The war in Indochina was not the World War III European type of war that the U.S. had prepared for. It was jungle warfare.

The Vietcong fought by using guerilla tactics. Surprise was the most important element in their strategy. Small groups hid in the jungles, or in tunnels that wove everywhere beneath the jungle floor. The jungle was the natural turf of the Vietnamese, and they used it as camouflage, shelter, and staging ground. They would attack suddenly, and then – just as quickly – withdraw, often without trace. Their use of booby traps, camouflaged pits containing sharp, pointed bamboo stakes, and mines not only took a heavy physical toll on their opponents, but took a psychological one as well, for American soldiers felt helpless and trapped in the face of these hidden dangers.

Given these circumstances, the three branches of the U.S. military decided in 1965 to reactivate their respective war dog programs. Conditions in Vietnam were not unlike those of the Pacific theater in World War II, where dogs had played a critical role in helping soldiers navigate the jungle. It was hoped that the U.S. dogs in Vietnam could provide an early warning system for ambushes, mines, and booby traps.

SENTRY DOGS

An attack in 1965 on Da Nang air base was the catalyst the Air Force needed to reactivate its sentry dog program. Several weeks after the attack, they shipped 40 handlers and 40 dogs to three air bases in Vietnam. The dogs quickly proved their effectiveness, and the Air Force increased its German shepherd sentry dog population to 476 over the next two years.

NEMO, THE GERMAN SHEPHERD SENTRY

Nemo, an 85-pound black-and-tan German shepherd, was a veteran sentry dog when he was shipped to Vietnam in January, 1966. He had joined the U.S. Air Force two years earlier, when he was one-and-a-half years old. He completed an eight-week training course at Lackland Sentry Dog Training School in San Antonio, Texas, and was assigned to an air base near Washington, D.C. He made the trip to Vietnam with a large group of other dog teams, and was assigned to security at Tan Son Nhut Air Base and to Airman 2nd Class Bob Thorneburg, who was to be his handler.

Tan Son Nhut, located just northwest of Saigon, was the largest air base in South Vietnam. Originally designed for 3,000 people, 25,000 people lived there and the population swelled to 50,000 during the day as people came to work. With this many civilians and soldiers coming into and out of the base every day, it was extremely difficult to maintain tight security.

By this time in the war, the Vietcong had begun focusing on infiltrating and attacking U.S. air bases. In February, three attempts were made on the air base at Pleiku, followed by ones at Bien Hoa and later Tan Son Nhut. The Vietcong, frustrated by acutely sensitive sentry dogs, began smearing their bodies with a garlic-like herb to disguise their smell. When this didn't work, they tried shelling kennel areas at various bases, in order to kill the offending sentries. This failed too.

But, on December 4, 1966, the Vietcong hit their mark at Tan Son Nhut. In the early morning hours, several sentry dogs stationed around the base gave an alert and warning. They had detected a group of 60-75 Vietcong about 100 yards outside the camp's perimeter.

Airman 2nd Class Leroy E. Marsh released his dog, Rebel, who was quickly killed in a hail of bullets. But the distraction that Rebel caused gave Marsh enough time to radio for help and to move to another sentry post several hundred yards away.

About an hour later, another sentry dog, named Cubby, alerted. His handler released him, and Cubby was shot too.

Just before dawn, a third sentry dog, named Toby, sensed the enemy. The Vietcong opened fire, killing Toby. His handler returned the fire, killing one of the enemy. Another handler chased a group of Vietcong who retreated and hid. Security police radioed their whereabouts to a central command post, so all units could prepare for an attack. Thirteen Vietcong tried to reach the main aircraft parking ramp, but were gunned down by security police hiding in a machine gun bunker. Other police closed off the perimeter of the base so that the enemy couldn't escape. By daybreak, security believed that all of the Vietcong infiltrators had either been killed or captured. Search patrols, which in the daylight did not include dogs, found nothing.

Three airmen and three dogs had been killed in the early morning attack, so the handlers and sentry dogs who went on duty that evening were a quiet, somber group. Everyone knew that there was still a good chance that Vietcong intruders were hiding inside the base, waiting for the cover of nightfall to try again.

Thorneburg and his dog Nemo were assigned guard duty near an old Vietnamese cemetery not too far from the airplane runways. Early in the night, Nemo alerted. Thorneburg released him, and the dog charged forward. Thorneburg heard shots being fired, and then he heard Nemo howling with pain. Thorneburg radioed in for back-up and began shooting. He killed one Vietcong soldier before being hit in the shoulder, falling to the ground.

Nemo had been shot in the head, but, despite his serious wound, crawled over to his master, covering him with his body. When back-up support reached Thorneburg and the dog, Nemo refused to let anyone get near his handler. He was finally pulled away, and both man and dog were taken back to the base for treatment for their wounds.

Meanwhile, sentry dog patrols continued sweeping the base. They located a team of four Vietcong, who were shot and killed. A second sweep found four more Vietcong who had been hiding underground. They too were killed. The attackers had finally been eradicated. Thanks to Nemo's alert, no more lives had been lost that night at Tan Son Nhut air base.

Nemo had been shot under his right eye, with the bullet exiting through his mouth. The base veterinarian, Lt. Raymond Hutson, couldn't save the sight in the dog's eye, but he did save his life. He performed many skin grafts on Nemo's face to restore the dog's appearance. But Nemo could no longer be an effective sentry dog, and in June, 1967, he was sent home to the U.S. with honors. (Thorneburg was taken to a hospital in Japan to recuperate, and also returned home with honors.)

Nemo survived the 24-hour flight home, touching down in Japan, Hawaii, and California. At each stop, he was treated like a hero and examined by Air Force vets who wanted to be sure he was comfortable. He spent the rest of his life at Lackland Air Force Base in Texas, in a kennel near the veterinary facility. A sign with his name and serial number described his heroism at Tan Son Nhut. He served as an Air Force dog recruiter, making appearances on television and helping the Air Force generate dog donations for the war effort. He died in 1973 at the age of 11 from a combination of his war wounds and old age.

PROBLEMS AS WELL AS SUCCESS

Meanwhile, the army began sending sentry dogs over to Vietnam in 1965. By 1966, they were organized as the 212th Military Police Company, composed of 250 men and 200 dogs, who were responsible for guarding 15 different locations. The dogs frustrated attempts by the Vietcong to infiltrate air bases at Pleiku, Bien Hoa, Phan Rang, Qui Nhon, and Ban Me Thot.

Despite the successes of sentry dogs, there was a growing problem. The Air Force was training the dogs to be the most vicious animals possible, in the hope that they would be not only physical deterrents to danger but give a morale boast to soldiers as well. Sometimes the dogs, who were trained to kill on command, turned on the wrong people – including veterinarians, kennel clean-up personnel, and soldiers trying to rescue the dogs' fallen masters. In addition, when their handlers completed their tour of duty and left Vietnam, their new handlers had a very difficult time convincing the dogs of who was boss.

HANS, THE GERMAN SHEPHERD SENTRY

John Burnam had just that difficulty when he became a sentry dog handler in January, 1967. He had spent part of the previous year as an infantryman in Vietnam, and then he had been shipped to a hospital in Okinawa to recover from a serious knee injury caused when he fell on a punji stake. When he learned about an opportunity to become a sentry dog handler, he jumped at the chance, remembering his love of dogs as a child.

His first assignment was to guard an army ammunition supply depot on Okinawa called the 267th Chemical Company. Upon arriving at the dog kennel on his first day at the depot, he was overwhelmed by the dogs. Many of them growled at him and hurled themselves at the fencing which separated the kennel rooms. Whenever Burnam moved close to a dog, it would snarl. It was hard for him to imagine that he would ever be able to control one of these animals.

Burnam was assigned to Hans, the biggest German shepherd in the kennel. Each dog was taught to listen to the commands of a single master only and since Hans had had a previous dog handler, Burnam had to begin the difficult task of getting to know Hans and encouraging him to transfer his allegiance from his former master to his new one. At first, Burnam didn't touch Hans, who still growled from behind his kennel fence every time Burnam came near. Over time, Burnam's fear subsided, and the two grew used to each other.

But the day the platoon sergeant told Burnam to take Hans out of his kennel for the first time, the fledgling dog handler was scared. By the end of that morning, however, Burnam and Hans were marching around the training yard in concert, with Burnam in control.

Hans had been trained in all the skills that a sentry dog required in order to do his job, but he needed a human master to make him perform. At first he was slow to obey Burnam, but gradually he became more responsive to his new handler, who started training him by using voice commands only. Eventually, Burnam graduated to using hand signals as instructions for the dog to follow. Sentry dog teams worked at night, and hand signals were effective when it was important to be silent.

But the most important, and scary, part of training was yet to come. About a month after meeting Hans, Burnam began training him to obey commands to attack. Burnam hadn't yet worked on duty and had never witnessed a sentry dog attack, so his first experience of it frightened him. All the members of the platoon lined up with their dogs. A soldier – outfitted in a heavy, padded, burlap suit and a face mask – entered the area. The sergeant ordered the first dog handler to give his dog the command to attack. Burnam couldn't believe the speed and power with which the animal attacked the man, trying to bite his throat and even knocking him down. The dog repeatedly sank his teeth into the suit, shaking his head from side to side as he did so.

By the time it was Burnam's turn to demonstrate his power over Hans, he was nervous. "Get him," Burnam ordered his dog, and Hans moved so fast that Burnam couldn't hold on to the leash. Before Burnam got the leash back in his hand, Hans had the padded man flat on the ground and was trying to bite off his leg. For the first time during the entire training exercise, the much put-upon soldier began yelling to have the dog called off.

"Out, out!" Burnam cried, giving the command for Hans to back off. But it took several tries and yanks on the leash before Hans finally let go his vice-like grip on the man's leg. And even then, Burnam had to work hard to keep Hans away from the fortunately heavily clad soldier.

The whole thing had taken less than a minute, but it left Burnam exhausted. Hans' gums were bleeding, and he was so tense that Burnam realized the dog would have killed the man if he hadn't been called off. However, since Hans had done as commanded, Burnam praised him.

Not too long after that, Burnam and Hans began active sentry duty. But, as much as Burnam grew to love Hans, he quickly became bored with guarding the munitions depot in Okinawa. As his obligatory 12-month tour of duty came to a close in March, 1967, Burnam made an unusual choice. He re-enlisted for another year of service in Vietnam.

THE PATROL DOG SOLUTION

The problems that Burnam faced in training Hans were not uncommon. The sentry dogs at the 267th Chemical Company in Okinawa were muzzled when they rode in trucks, for example, because they always seemed to want to attack each other or any person who came too close. The vicious nature of the sentry dogs was not always controllable, and harmful incidents were not always averted. In Saigon, for instance, a sentry dog was riding in a jeep that passed another open army car with several soldiers inside. The dog bit and mangled the ear of one of the soldiers, without any provocation.

Realizing they had a problem, the Air Force hired the Metropolitan Police Department of Washington, D.C., in 1968 to train a new type of sentry dog – the patrol dog. The patrol dog was trained differently from the sentry dog so he could work with more people and in a variety of situations. The patrol dog did not wear a muzzle and did his job off-leash, although his handler could order him to attack if necessary. These broader capabilities meant that patrol dogs could also serve as escorts and perform crowd control.

Though both the Air Force and the Strategic Air Command agreed that patrol dogs were superior to sentry dogs, only limited numbers actually served in Vietnam after 1968. By that time, the air bases had so many people on them that the dogs couldn't do their jobs effectively. A year later U.S. troops began their planned gradual withdrawal, and fewer dogs were needed.

Chapter Seven

Walking Point: Scout Dogs in Vietnam

The Training Regimen

The Marines and the Army both decided to reactivate their scout dog teams in 1965, but trained handlers and dogs weren't ready for combat in Vietnam until 1966. There was a shortage of qualified dogs, compounded by the fact that donations of suitable dogs to the American military were low because the war was so politically explosive. There was also a lack of qualified instructors.

Scout dogs underwent 12 weeks of training in Fort Benning, Georgia, before being sent to Vietnam. Handlers remained with the dogs throughout the entire period. Basic obedience took up the first two weeks. In addition to being taught basic commands such as heel, sit, down, stay, and crawl, dogs were taught to obey at the sound of a voice or by hand signal. Dog and handler got to know each other during this period. This was the critical time when the handler established himself as the dog's master or ran the risk that the dog would not perform the way he should.

At the end of the first two weeks, field instruction began, which taught the dog to "alert" to enemy presence. No two dogs alert the same way, so it was critical for handlers to learn their dog's signs well enough so that there was no mistaking the danger signal. Many dogs alerted by pointing forward while their ears stood upright. For others, the alert would be that the hair on their backs would stand up. One army dog called Major actually crossed his ears when alerting, and another named Eric walked on his hind legs. Although a dog probably didn't know whether he was alerting to an enemy force or a weapons cache, his alerts could vary in intensity very visibly. The stronger the alert, the greater the immediate danger would be. Once something menacing was detected, the dog was taught to give a silent warning, since barking would alert an enemy.

Early in training, lessons took place during daylight, but when the dog was good enough, he would be taught at night. This required the human handler, with his relatively poor night vision, to become even more reliant on the dog.

The man–dog teams spent three days training in a simulated Vietcong village, in order to learn how to function in the same conditions they would experience in Vietnam. Unfortuately, one thing that the trainers at Fort Benning failed to consider was the fact the most northern Vietnamese villages would contain civilians as well as Vietcong soldiers. Dogs trained in this reproduction village therefore alerted to both civilians and soldiers alike once they were in the real

Vietnam, which made it difficult for American soldiers to figure out who to fire at. Another reality not addressed in training was the fact that many villages contained livestock and domestic animals, which often distracted the dogs.

The final phase of scout dog training came in the eleventh week, when the teams performed under simulated combat conditions. They crossed obstacles, scouted rice paddies, navigated through swamps, caves, and tunnels, worked from a boat, and scouted through simulated villages and jungles. The instructors, about 40 percent of whom had served in Vietnam, made the final judgement on whether the dog was ready to go to Vietnam.

The dog's success depended in large part on his handler. Although, officially, handlers were supposed to be volunteers who liked dogs, there was a shortage of such people, which meant that many soldiers without any sensitivity to animals were assigned to the job.

The Air Force began training scout dogs alongside the Army in 1966, after they realized that defending only the perimeter of their air bases was not enough to ensure victory against battalion-sized attacks. Within three months, Air Force scout dogs were included in units who were ordered to patrol outside air bases in active search of the enemy.

Although many scout dogs and handlers were trained at Fort Benning, probably just as many received training on-the-job in Vietnam. The scout dog program grew to over 1,000 canines by 1967.

In 1968, a scout dog demonstration was staged by the 47th Scout Dog Platoon for 2nd Brigade commanders. Rusty Allen and his dog Sig were chosen to demonstrate, and some platoon members were concerned that the officers would think all scout dogs were infallible since Sig was so good. However, toward the end of the demonstration, Sig lunged on his leash at a decoy, which caused Allen to fall face-first on his helmet and break his nose.

Despite this mishap, the demonstration was so successful that the Brigade Commander requested a written procedure on the proper use and deployment of Scout Dogs. By 1969, 22 Army war dog platoons and four Marine dog platoons were operating. About 1,400 dogs were responsible for patrolling South Vietnam, which is over 65,000 square miles in size. Most of the dog platoons, however, were concentrated in the area surrounding Saigon, where the majority of Communist hideouts and supply stations were located.

CLIPPER, THE GERMAN SHEPHERD SCOUT

In March, 1967 John Burnam re-enlisted for a second tour of duty in Vietnam and volunteered for the 44th Infantry Scout Dog Platoon. He and his scout dog platoon were posted to Dau Tieng, an army base located just to the northwest of Saigon.

His decision was unusual because becoming a scout dog handler meant you became a pointman. "Walking point" was one of the most dangerous jobs in South Vietnam. Pointmen walked ahead of their units, scouting for the enemy. Usually, the Vietcong, who had the advantage of hiding in the jungle, spotted a pointman first. A pointman with a dog, however, turned the tables. A dog's acute sense of smell and hearing meant that a dog handler could find the enemy before the enemy found him. Burnam figured that he would rather take his chances with a well-trained scout dog leading the way than by trying to survive in Vietnam on only his own instincts and experience.

A BLACK AND TAN GERMAN SHEPHERD.

Burnam's first dog with the Scout Dog Platoon was a German shepherd named Timber. After several uneventful missions, Burnam and Timber were both wounded when their patrol was ambushed on a mission outside Dau Tieng in May, 1967. Burnam's wounds weren't serious, but Timber had been traumatized by the attack. Although he recovered physically, the dog no longer showed any spunk or aggressiveness. Burnam decided he needed a new scout.

He chose a dog from the kennel named Clipper, with whom he felt an instant bond. The German shepherd was big, weighing 80 pounds, and had a black and brown coat, big brown eyes, and tall pointed ears. He would let any American soldier pet him, but he was very aggressive toward any Vietnamese person.

Burnam and Clipper spent several weeks training and getting to know each other. Burnam set up mock scenarios inside the kennel compound so that he could find out how Clipper alerted to trip wires, booby traps, and the enemy – and at what distances and under which weather conditions.

Burnam knew that he and Clipper had to work as a tightly knit team because they were to serve as a silent early warning system for the patrol following them. Burnam's job was to keep focused on the dog, reading his alerts. In turn, the patrol behind them would watch out for Burnam and Clipper.

On Thanksgiving Day, 1967, Burnam and Clipper were assigned to be part of a point platoon for a battalion-sized mission close to the Cambodian border. They were the only scout dog team in the platoon.

As was often the case, Burnam didn't know anyone else in the platoon where he'd be working for the next few days. In a way it was better, he felt, because becoming attached to people made it more difficult when there were casualties. Anyway, even back among the other scout dog handlers at the base camp, Burnam considered Clipper to be his best friend. Burnam never went out with other handlers on missions, so, although he and his colleagues were friendly, they didn't develop the bonds that usually are made during combat. Burnam relied instead on the companionship of Clipper, which made their working relationship all the stronger.

The platoon split up into small groups for the helicopter ride into the jungle. Once they were in the air, Clipper leaned out of the helicopter's open doorway, enjoying the cool wind on his face. He leaned farther and farther forward, while Burnam strained to hold the leash. He would yank the dog back, but Clipper would always head for the doorway again. After several turns at this game, Burnam gathered some slack leash in his fist. Clipper started to lean out of the door again, and this time Burnam released the slack, causing the German shepherd to pitch forward and almost fall out of the chopper. The dog's hair stood straight up, his eyes got huge, and he dropped quickly on all fours then slunk back toward Burnam. Sometimes dog training was impromptu.

When the platoon hit the ground, they moved away from the landing clearing. The scout-dog team was assigned to the lead squad, and two infantrymen were assigned to cover Burnam and Clipper. Burnam told the two soldiers to follow far enough behind them so that Clipper had full scent capability in the direction they were traveling, and not to come between them and their goal unless Burnam gave them a signal that it was okay to do so.

Clipper first alerted to some fresh enemy footprints, but not until several hours later did his next alert come. The army unit was in a forest with clear visibility, but Burnam couldn't see anything out of the ordinary. Clipper's alert was strong, however, so he motioned for the platoon unit leader, who agreed to send a rifle team forward to search the area. They reported a large clearing, but no sign of the enemy. As they moved across the clearing, though, Clipper gave the strongest alert of the day. His ears stood upright, and he bent his head to one side. Again, the platoon leader sent men forward, and they discovered a heavily traveled path, which must have been a branch of the Ho Chi Minh trail.

They continued to move forward through the clearing, but Clipper alerted again, with the muscles on his back growing especially tense. Burnam signaled back to the men behind him that there might be trouble, but for some reason this time the platoon leader disregarded the warning. Burnam was ordered to move ahead, but Clipper didn't want to, and started side-stepping. Suddenly, shots rang out from the tree line ahead. Burnam and Clipper dropped down, as did all the men behind them, searching for the sniper. Someone in the platoon decided to fire over Burnam's head toward the trees, and then everyone began shooting. But there was no return of fire, and, after a little while, the platoon closed in on the tree line.

Once under cover of the trees, the soldiers began milling around, waiting for their next order. A lieutenant came toward Burnam, and told him that a bunker had been spotted up ahead. He asked Burnam if he and Clipper would check it out with him. Burnam agreed and then the lieutenant led the way toward the bunker, with Clipper and Burnam following closely behind.

Shortly after they passed the last men in the platoon, Clipper alerted into the trees. But Burnam ignored it because of the confusion surrounding them, and because the lieutenant was walking ahead of them, obscuring Clipper's scent line.

The jungle became dark and thick with vegetation. The lieutenant led, hacking a path through the undergrowth, with Burnam and Clipper following.

Suddenly, at point blank range, guns were shooting at them. The lieutenant's body hurled into Burnam's, knocking him to the ground. The dog rolled on top of them. Burnam's helmet came off and clattered away, but he held on firmly to Clipper's leash. About 20 yards behind them, the Americans opened fire.

Burnam and Clipper crawled behind a tree, but they were caught in the crossfire. Bullets raked the ground in all directions. The Vietcong were entrenched about 15 feet away from Burnam, close enough for him to hear them whispering from their foxholes. In the commotion, Burnam's gun had become clogged with dirt. He hadn't packed any grenades, and he was still without his helmet. There was nothing he could do but pray he wouldn't be seen. Clipper must have figured that out too – he stayed quiet and calm.

Meanwhile, the American soldiers were getting closer and closer to the Vietcong, and began blasting them with artillery. Throughout it all, machine guns continued to shred the vegetation around them.

Burnam felt something touch his foot. Frightened, he turned to look, and saw an American soldier who had come to cover him so that they could make their way back to safety. No words were spoken.

Burnam turned on his belly with Clipper and began inching back toward friendly lines. He heard an M16 being fired, and then the sound of a grenade, but he kept moving ahead.

They passed a dead Vietnamese hanging from a tree by a foot caught in the branches. Later, Burnam realized that this was the scent Clipper had alerted to earlier and they had ignored because of the commotion.

Shortly after Burnam and Clipper made it safely behind American lines, the shooting stopped. The Vietcong had either fled or been wiped out. Burnam watched as the lieutenant's dead, limp body was carried away on a poncho. He learned that the soldier who had come to cover them and help them retreat had also been shot.

In all, six men were killed and 11 wounded in the firefight. Almost all of the casualties had occurred while the soldiers had been milling around, waiting for the scout dog team and lieutenant to check out the bunker. The Vietcong had set up the platoon by baiting it with the first sniper.

As he reviewed the events of the day, Burnam couldn't believe that he and Clipper had escaped harm. Clipper had been a silent and brave soldier, and many troop members came by to thank the dog for his good work.

On- or Off-Leash?

Another element that affected the scout dog's performance was whether he worked on- or off-leash. Although World War II experience had taught the military that scout dogs could be effective off-leash, early in the Vietnam war, all scout dogs were trained using 15-foot leashes. An important element of this training was for the dog to learn to always allow a little bit of slack in the leash so as not to drag the handler. The idea was that eventually the man-dog team would work together as though the leash were invisible. Although the leash provided the handler with better control of the dog, with the need for fewer voice and hand signals, the proximity of handler to dog meant that the soldier was in greater danger should the dog discover the enemy or a booby trap.

By 1968, dogs were being trained to work off-leash. So that the handler could more easily read the dog's alert from a greater distance, the scout was taught to sit while in the presence of danger. Working with an off-leash dog meant that the handler had two hands free and a greater distance between himself and possible attack. He also didn't have to worry about the leash getting tangled in vegetation. But ultimately the handler could choose whether to work on- or off-leash with his dog. It was a matter not only of training, but also of confidence.

RINGO, THE GERMAN SHEPHERD SURVIVOR

Like most handlers in the 44th Scout Dog Platoon, Roger Jones worked off-leash with Ringo, his German shepherd. Jones, who had won the award as best trainee during his session at scout dog school in Fort Benning, preferred it that way. But on a mission in June 1967, his dog Ringo bolted away from him during a firefight with the Vietcong. Having a dog run away was very unusual, and Jones' superiors were so angry that they filed a report charging the dog handler with negligence. Fortunately, the charge was not pursued, since it could have resulted in Jones' being court-martialed.

Several weeks later, a story in the American army newspaper in Vietnam, *Stars and Stripes*, reported that a badly wounded dog had followed an American patrol into the Cu Chi base camp. The dog had taken a bullet in his jaw at close range. He was dehydrated and hungry. He had spent several days hiding in the jungle, evading the Vietcong. He was taken at first to the 38th Scout Dog Platoon based at Cu Chi, but his serial number didn't match with any of their dogs. A phone call to the 44th confirmed that the dog was Ringo.

The top brass seemed to soften towards Ringo, once they understood that his wound was probably what caused him to bolt. Jones and Ringo flew to Saigon, where a well-known military dental surgeon patched up the dog's wound. A month later, the pair returned to the platoon, so Ringo could complete his convalescence. Eventually, the only evidence of his ordeal was his tongue, which had a chunk missing from the right side where the bullet had passed through his jaw. Ringo was admired for his intelligence in finding his way to safety, and his courage in surviving his serious injury.

BACK AT BASE CAMP WITH MASCOTS

Between missions, scout dog teams spent their time at base camp, where the schedule was relaxed and the men could set their own pace. After breakfast, it was the handlers' job to feed the dogs, give them water, and clean the kennels.

Training to reinforce the dogs' skills occurred constantly. Soldiers would set up mock training scenarios to keep the dogs on their toes. One veteran reported that, at Camp Evans, training occurred every morning. They used captured enemy equipment and clothes as decoys, and sometimes included trip wires attached to a small explosive charge. If a dog hit the trip wire, it scared him so much that it usually didn't happen again. Exercises were repeated in different weather conditions to see how the dogs' performance would vary. The humidity, heat, denseness of vegetation, and ambient noise all affected the dogs. Try as they might, however, the soldiers couldn't replicate conditions outside the base camp, where they would be conducting their missions.

When work was finished for the day, handlers often played with their dogs. In fact, handlers spent many of their waking hours with the dogs, although the canines had to return to their kennels to sleep.

Apparently this wasn't enough, for the members of the 44th Scout Dog Platoon also had a mascot, a tiny mutt that someone had brought from the U.S. She was named 44, and she had a shiny black coat, a long nose, and floppy ears. Unlike the working dogs, she was free to roam the compound. 44 was killed when she was run over on a dirt road in front of the yard. The men buried her under a nearby rubber tree.

Not too long afterward, a handler brought another mascot into camp – a tiny Vietnamese puppy he had found out on a mission. This dog was no bigger than a squirrel, and he had short white hair. The men named him Hardcore, because he had so much energy. For several months, he roamed all over camp, chewing on anything he could find. However, Hardcore was killed when he ran foul of one of the German shepherds.

The 47th Infantry Platoon Scout Dog also had a mascot, a tiny, black, mixed-breed puppy named Flexible. Jonathan Wahl picked her up when she was running loose at Bien Hoa Army camp, a stray who was going to be put to sleep by the Vietnamese. After her rescue by Wahl, she became very spoiled by the soldiers. American soldiers loved to indulge their mascots in ways that would have been harmful to the working dogs. As one member of the 47th wrote home about Flexible:

"The other night everyone kept giving her food until she got so stuffed she could not move. Her stomach was bulging out and she was laying there in agony. She has recovered since however. It is really strange to see her along with our big dogs. Our big dogs are very curious and do not seem to be able to figure her out."

A year later, Flexible delivered puppies, which were clearly part German shepherd.

Dogs and their handlers were assigned to go out on missions based on a system called the Rotation. Dog teams were listed on a board in an order determined by the commanding officer. As calls came in from infantry divisions for teams, the pairs at the top of the board would go out first. When a team returned from a mission, they would drop to the bottom of the board so they would have time to rest until it was their turn to go out again. Missions were typically from three to five days long, but varied depending on circumstances. Despite the risks of walking point, many handlers felt fortunate to be able to spend so much time at base camp instead of out in the bush. During the course of a year-long tour, a dog handler would be out on missions from 90 to 120 days, whereas an infantryman might spend 300 days in the bush. As the website for the 47th Infantry Platoon Scout Dog eloquently puts it: "Dog handlers, for the most part, were grateful to be dog handlers. Dog handlers as a group were very appreciative and respectful of the infantryman who had to lay it on the line every day. We were blessed with our heroic K-9 friends (our protectors)."

POLAR BEAR, THE WHITE GERMAN SHEPHERD SCOUT
Paul Morgan first met Polar Bear, a white German shepherd, at Fire Base Diana near the Cambodian border in early January, 1970. Polar Bear was vicious, and he growled at anyone who came near where he was staked out at a bunker. Two days before Morgan met him, Polar Bear's handler had been killed when he and the rest of his infantry scout dog platoon had been flushing out Vietcong from a bunker complex. The same fire that killed the handler had wounded Polar Bear in the face and shoulders.

A German Shepherd

Both had been evacuated from the battle scene, but no one could spare the time to care for Polar Bear's wounds. Someone tied him to a piece of artillery, but he was given little to eat and he had no relief from the pain. He paced back and forth furiously, and wouldn't let the soldiers who threw him scraps and garbage from the mess hall come close.

Although Morgan wasn't assigned to a dog platoon, he had worked with dogs in the army for ten years, and knew how valuable each and every dog could be. So rather than dismiss Polar Bear, he tried approaching the dog, who tried to break his lead and attack the soldier.

Morgan wasn't afraid. "Sit and stay," he commanded.

He let Polar Bear off his leash, but he was ready to shoot the dog if he tried to attack again. Polar Bear seemed to sense this, and obeyed. Morgan took off his helmet, turned it over, and emptied cold water into it. Polar Bear growled, drank some of the cold water, wagged his tail, and finished it off.

"Watch that white dog, sir," said some soldiers who suddenly appeared. "He's a bad dude."

But Morgan found a medic who could treat the dog. Morgan held Polar Bear, who was growling and snapping with pain, while the frightened doctor tended the animal's wounds. Then Morgan attached Polar Bear to a piece of rope, and led the dog around the base as he went about his business, picking up orders and maps. Morgan found some meat and bread for Polar Bear, who was starved and ate it as fast as he could.

The soldier decided that he needed to return Polar Bear to his scout dog unit, so he hopped on a helicopter with the dog and flew out to the field. The veterinarian seemed surprised to see Polar Bear, who had been listed as killed in action along with his handler. "He's salvage equipment, sir," the vet told the soldier.

Morgan knew what that meant – the wounded dog would be put down because of his injuries. Morgan turned away, taking Polar Bear with him. "I'm en route to Saigon," Morgan lied, "and I'll turn him in for you."

The veterinarian went along with it. He went into the kennel area, and came back with a water-proof bag filled with ten pounds of dry dog meal. "You'll need this," he said, adding, "Thanks."

Morgan and Polar Bear flew back to Fire Base Diana. Fire bases were temporary artillery bases established to support ground operations in a given area. Polar Bear took up guard duty at Morgan's bunker, crawling under Morgan's cot at first. Later, he slept on Morgan's bed, snoring with his head on the pillow. Soon he became friendly with anyone who liked dogs. He got his own cot, and slept for almost all of every day. Though he didn't like Army dog rations, he ate plenty of rice, bread, meat, and dry meal. In two weeks, he gained 20 pounds. Polar Bear was recovering from his trauma in the field, both physically and emotionally.

Fire Base Diana was a new base which the North Vietnamese Army was not happy about. Bunkers were half built, and barbed wire had been up for only three days, when Morgan and the 900 soldiers posted there got word that 1,500 Vietcong troops were about to attack. The area surrounding the base was a maze of tunnels which the Vietcong used as troop barracks, hospitals, and supply caches. And though the Vietcong were rarely visible, the many mines and booby traps they left were clear signs of their presence.

The sound of incoming mortar rounds began late in the evening on January 25, and Morgan could tell from the sound that the enemy was only 200 yards outside the perimeter of the base. In short order, 60 mortar rounds destroyed the main command center, all of the long-range radios, and two of their six howitzers. Eight soldiers were dead and 12 wounded in a matter of minutes.

Morgan, a major who was responsible for deploying artillery, gunships, and jet fighter-bombers to support Vietnamese and U.S. troops, got on the radio in his backpack to call for help. "Sierra, this is Mike," he said. "NVA inside the wire. Lady Diana is in trouble. Over."

Soon, a platoon of helicopter gunships was flying overhead.

Meanwhile, Vietcong were running straight at the wire in a suicical frontal assault. Morgan, his assistant Sam Parsons, and a radio operator named Rosario couldn't believe what they were seeing. The men and Polar Bear, who sat on his master's left foot, watched as two sappers made their way through the wire with satchel charges, and then were shot down by machine guns. Two rockets from the overhead helicopters hit the area where the enemy seemed to be concentrated. Soldiers continued firing grenades and machine guns at enemy soldiers visible in the light of flares.

Things seemed to be coming under control, when suddenly Polar Bear alerted. Morgan, Parsons, and Rosario squatted down, but they couldn't see anything. There was a trench near them that led to the command post, but the men couldn't make anything out. Polar Bear started to bark, and Rosario and Morgan both fired into the blackness. A few minutes later, support planes dropped some flares so the gunships could strafe the enemy. Morgan saw two dead enemy soldiers in a trench only thirty feet away. Rosario had killed them when he fired blindly into the darkness. "I just fired where the dog pointed me," he said.

The enemy assault on Fire Base Diana was a failure. The Vietcong began to withdraw about midnight, leaving behind 42 dead and probably suffering at least 100 casualties. Morgan and the other soldiers were feeling good about their work, when the enemy began firing more mortars on the base as they withdrew. Morgan was hit and went down.

Polar Bear stood over him until Morgan passed out from the pain. The next morning Morgan was airlifted out. Only two days later, Polar Bear was killed by mortar fire as he was walking around the base. He was buried with full military honors.

Chapter Eight

Searching for Trip Wires and Booby Traps

WHY MINE DETECTION DOGS WERE NECESSARY

Booby traps and mines were among the most frightening aspects of fighting for soldiers in Vietnam. They accounted for 10 percent of deaths and nearly 20 percent of casualties. But numbers don't tell the whole story. Part of the effectiveness of such hidden explosives was their ability to undermine the soldier's feeling of control and to damage his psyche. The Vietcong were masters at hiding the devices so that it was extremely difficult to detect them. They were also diabolical in aiming them at the face or groin, and for many American soldiers the prospect of such disfigurement was worse than death.

All of the technological advances made in mine detection since World War II were of little use with the crudely-made traps used by the Vietcong. Punji pits, for example, were holes set with sharpened bamboo stakes, the points of which were often covered with feces that would turn even superficial wounds into infected nightmares. The cruder the trap, the more difficult it was to find.

The use of mines and booby traps was so much more pervasive in Vietnam than it was in World War II that the army decided to try once again to train mine detection dogs. M-dogs, as they were called, hadn't proved reliable in World War II for various reasons. The distractions of large-scale conflicts, with their masses of dead bodies and burning vehicles, made it difficult for M-dogs to concentrate on their job. More importantly, the military hadn't found a strong enough motivation to reward the dogs for finding mines. Simply feeding them something to eat each time they found a mine wasn't producing reliable results. Motivating the dogs through fear – for instance, by giving them a mild electric shock when they located a mine – was also, not surprisingly, unsuccessful.

So, in 1967, the U.S. Army Limited Warfare Laboratory decided to attempt M-dog training one more time. They contracted with a civilian company called Behavior Systems, Inc. (BSI), based in North Carolina, to try to motivate the dogs using food in a slightly different way. The day before training started, the dogs on the course were not fed. The first day of training, a dog's food ration was split up and placed on top of a number of visible mines. The dog was allowed to eat each time he found a mine. Gradually, as the days went by, the food was placed on only some of the mines. Eventually, the trainer held the food and rewarded his dog with it only after he could sit in front of a hidden mine.

The goal was to have the dog find 90 percent of the devices. He was trained to find them whether they were buried six inches deep, elevated up to five feet off the ground, or located within 10 feet to the side of the route of travel. The dogs were usually trained to work off-leash and could range up to 300 feet ahead of the handler. In the best conditions, downwind of a light breeze, dogs could make detections 100 to 200 feet away. The dogs were also taught to detect trip wires and booby traps, which were carefully camouflaged on trees. Booby traps were easier for the dogs to detect than mines, since their smells were carried on the air.

Seven months after they started, Behavior Systems, Inc. had trained 14 dogs to detect mines, booby traps, and trip wires. The Army requested a demonstration, the results of which would determine whether BSI would receive a contract to train an additional 56 dogs for Vietnam. Since not all of the 12 Army spectators at the demonstration were receptive to the idea of mine detection dogs, the BSI personnel were somewhat nervous.

Under the supervision of Army men to ensure that no cheating took place, BSI built a trial obstacle course, complete with several mines, a tunnel, and a punji pit (although they did not fill it with sharpened bamboo stakes). The day of the demonstration – July 18, 1968 – was hot and muggy, ideal for replicating conditions in Vietnam. Six dogs performed that day, and all of them rose to the occasion. With each find, the spectators would gather around while the mine was dug up, for confirmation of a correct detection.

One of the observers remained skeptical, however, and saw his chance when a dog sat on the edge of the well-hidden punji pit. Before anyone could declare the detection correct, the colonel ordered everyone to stay put. He wanted to examine the pit himself, hoping, no doubt, to find evidence of foul play. He approached the seated dog, scouring the ground. As he got closer, he got down on all fours, carefully examining the dirt. Finally, nose-to-nose with the dog, the colonel stood up and declared that it was a false response – there was no pit. As he walked around the seated dog, he fell through the grasses and branches camouflaging the pit. Fortunately, only his pride was hurt.

Based on the success of these trials, the training of M-dogs continued. BSI also trained tunnel dogs in very similar ways, although no voice commands were used since the tunnels could contain the enemy. Tunnel dogs were trained to sit outside a tunnel when they found it, but never to enter it.

By April, 1969, 28 mine and tunnel dogs were included in the 60th Infantry Platoon which arrived in Vietnam at Cu Chi. Another 28 dogs were turned over to the Marines.

In real-life combat, the dogs initially proved very successful. Patrol leaders were asked to evaluate their contribution, and 85 percent said they believed the dogs enhanced security.

Not surprisingly, the dogs also often alerted to dangers not specified in their training. Mine dogs found Vietcong, and tunnel dogs found booby traps. This was equally true of scout dogs, who often alerted to trip wires and booby traps.

WOLF, THE GERMAN SHEPHERD VETERAN SCOUT DOG

Charlie Cargo arrived in Vietnam in 1970, and was assigned to the 48th Scout Dog Platoon stationed in Chu Lai. Like all soldiers newly arrived in Vietnam, Cargo was constantly struggling to figure out which end was up. The culture of Vietnam, combined with guerrilla warfare tactics, was overwhelming. Fortunately for Cargo, he was assigned to Wolf. Wolf, a mostly black German shepherd, was a veteran scout dog who could locate trip wires and traps up to one thousand yards away. He had

A BLACK AND TAN GERMAN SHEPHERD

an excellent track record, and he was Cargo's patient teacher over the next four weeks. A month into his tour of duty, Cargo and Wolf were out in the field. Here is Cargo's own account of what happened:

"We were nearing the summit of the barren slope when Wolf suddenly stopped and sat down.

" 'Come on, Wolfer, let's go,' I said hoarsely between gulps of air. But he refused to move. He just sat there, his big pink tongue hanging out of one side of his mouth. Now the slack man was breathing on the back of my neck. 'Damn, Cargo, let's go.' The grunts behind us were really starting to bunch up and we were still in the open.

" 'Then tell them to spread out and take what cover they can find,' I said, waving irritably behind my back with one hand for him to give me some space. I wasn't about to take my eyes off of Wolf. 'He's alerting to something.' I motioned for Wolf to return to me, then sent him out to do a second search. Personally, I didn't really believe there was anything to worry about. Just a few dry clumps of weeds up here, pitiful cover for anybody or anything.

"Now Wolf was back at the same spot on the hillside, sitting in the dirt just like before. In a low crouch, I moved up to his position and gave him a pat. 'Whassup, boy?' His head rolled lazily about on his shoulders as he cast me a casual glance. I splashed a little canteen water in a tin cup and held it under his chin. 'You just thirsty, Wolfer?' He ignored it. 'Well, you aren't sniffing the air or listening to anything. Stop worrying and let's go. Everything's O.K.'

"Meanwhile, the slack man was telling the troops to quit their whining and bitching. 'Shut up,' he hissed through closed teeth. 'The dog's onto something.'

"As the man spoke, I was in mid-stride and about to step around Wolf. Suddenly the dog wrenched his body sideways blocking me. 'Hey, it's OK, I'm only looking,' I whispered. And that was when he bit me.

"Those jaws of his were like a vice – a vice fitted with tiger teeth, which were now penetrating my right hand. It was such a shock it took a few seconds for the pain to sink in, and when it did, it was blinding. I was too surprised to scream. Flailing like a fish, I frantically tried to wrench my hand out of his mouth. Blood was starting to trickle down my wrist. . .time seemed to be standing still. Finally – mercifully, blessedly – he let go.

"Now I knew something was wrong. 'Well for crying out loud, what is it?' I blurted, trying to push down the urge to vomit as waves of agony began rolling up my arm. And then I saw it – a tripwire the thickness of a hair. Two feet in front of me. My knees began to shake as the realization of just how close I'd come to dying began to sink in – and how I would have taken Wolf with me."

Wolf had saved Cargo's life, and the lives of many men in the unit.

Over the year, through the course of daily life as well as during dangerous missions, Cargo's bond with Wolf deepened. They were inseparable, best friends as well as working partners. Cargo's mother even started including dog biscuits for Wolf in the care packages she sent to her son. The letters Cargo wrote back to his family sometimes included Wolf's signature – a muddy pawprint. "More than master and servant, more than brothers, we were of one heart and soul," Cargo said.

ON THE JOB TRAINING

As the war dragged on, mine and tunnel dogs became less effective. Trainers began to deviate from the original regimen laid out in BSI's training manual, and handlers became less experienced. As troops began gradually to withdraw, starting in 1969, some mine and tunnel dog teams migrated to scout dog platoons, often working together. As a result of all these variables, some dog teams were not successful, while others performed well. Often, training occurred not at home in the United States, but at base camp in Vietnam.

Some veterans felt that their dog, not their instructor, was their best teacher. John Burnam is an example of how successful a handler could be simply by understanding what he and his dog needed to work on, and then developing a training routine.

CLIPPER LEADS EVERYONE HOME

Within a short time after starting to work with Clipper in 1967, John Burnam decided that he needed to know more about how the dog would alert to a booby trap. He knew Clipper would never intentionally set off a trip wire, but he didn't know what signals Clipper would give when he came too close. On the day Burnam decided to begin trip wire training, he set up a fake trip wire in a grove of rubber trees inside the army compound. Burnam put Clipper on his leash, and began circling the area.

As they got closer to the wire, Clipper gave a weak alert, but he didn't stop walking. The wire touched the top of his head, and he began to duck under.

"No," said Burnam, pulling up firmly on the leash.

They tried it again and again, until finally Clipper stopped in front of the trip wire and sat down. Burnam was ecstatic and praised the dog lavishly. They continued practicing for several hours that day, and repeated the routine for the next week.

Burnam moved the wire to different places to see how Clipper's alerts might differ. He learned that if Clipper sensed the trip wire from a distance, he would walk around it. If he came directly upon it, Clipper would sit down in front of it.

As impressed as he was with his dog, Burnam still didn't know how Clipper would work in the thick jungle where most of their encounters with the enemy would take place. He got a chance to find out when he and Clipper were assigned to another mission, this time with an infantry battalion.

The Vietcong had been building up around the base camp, their forces frequently attacking American airstrips with mortars. The two-day mission by the platoon was to be a sweep to find and destroy hidden Vietcong outposts.

The platoon flew to the designated starting point in helicopters. Within their first hour on the ground, a heavy rain began. The jungle was so dense that soldiers with machetes had to hack a trail through the undergrowth. Eventually, the vegetation got lighter, and Burnam volunteered to take the point.

Soon, Clipper alerted, but a fire team sent ahead didn't find anything. Fifty yards farther on, Clipper alerted again. This time an advance patrol reported finding a Vietcong base camp directly ahead. No shots had been fired by the enemy, so the Americans assumed that the Vietcong had either left the camp, or were hiding nearby.

The scout dog team entered the base camp with other members of the first squad and began cautiously investigating. Clipper alerted to a clump of branches on the ground. It was a fifty gallon drum of marijuana. Clipper had found the Vietcong's pot stash – which made him pretty popular with some of the soldiers.

The next day, Burnam's platoon joined a sister platoon which had suffered casualties when they were hit by command-detonated mines that the Vietcong had planted among the trees in a rubber plantation. The combined platoons were to sweep through the small villages around the plantation, looking for hidden Vietcong.

They searched one hamlet, but couldn't find any Vietnamese guerillas, only old people and children. Feelings were running high because of the soldiers hit by the mines, and everyone began to appear suspicious to the Americans.

Finally, they prepared to move out for the final sweep of their mission. They were only a mile away from Dau Tieng base camp, and home felt close. But, as Burnam and Clipper passed between some trees, Burnam heard a huge explosion. Then he heard the sounds of a soldier in agony. He quickly crawled over to the man, whose legs and feet were blood-soaked. Burnam saw a broken trip wire attached to a stick in the ground – it was a booby trap.

After the injured soldier was flown out, Burnam stepped forward. He knew it was time to see just how good Clipper was at detecting trip wires, or many more people would be killed. He told the platoon leader that he and the dog would be taking the lead, and he headed forward. Behind him, the platoon leader ordered the soldiers to go single-file. Clipper was now in charge of leading the men safely home to Dau Tieng base camp.

Burnam kept his eyes glued on Clipper's ears as the dog guided his handler forward. Clipper alerted faintly to the left, hesitated, and then moved right. Burnam couldn't see into the knee-high grass, and he didn't see anything at eye level, so he kept on going. Again and again, Clipper would give an alert in one direction, and then move in the opposite one. Since Burnam couldn't see anything out of the ordinary, he decided to stop worrying about why Clipper was weaving such an elaborate path. He did know that there had been no more explosions, and that they were getting close to home.

Every so often, Burnam was ordered from behind to stop. Behind him, the column of American soldiers snaked through the grass.

Just outside the wire of the Dau Tieng base camp, Clipper and Burnam stopped to wait for the rest of the platoon to catch up. As the soldiers passed them by, some of them smiled. The platoon leader showed up and thanked Burnam for getting them through all the booby traps. Burnam, of course, hadn't seen any booby traps.

The lieutenant told him that the first time Clipper had changed directions, one of the soldiers had seen a grenade tied to the base of tree. After that, whenever Clipper veered off, the men would look for a trap. They stopped to mark them, so that they could be detonated after the company was out of the area.

The lieutenant hugged Clipper and the dog shook hands with him. The lieutenant also thanked Burnam, and said that he would recommend both man and dog for the Bronze Star Medal. It was the highest compliment Burnam had ever been paid for doing his job, but he knew that Clipper deserved all the credit. He gave his dog a bear hug and lots of loving words. His trust and confidence in Clipper grew immeasurably that day.

TRACKER DOGS

One of the hallmarks of the Vietcong strategy was to ambush and then disappear quickly into the night. An early example of this was an attack on Bien Hoa Air Base in October, 1964, when the Vietcong destroyed six newly arrived American B-57 jet bombers and damaged another 20. Although search parties immediately pursued the 100 attackers, not a single enemy was found. In another instance in 1967, Vietcong guerillas stole into a fishing village in the dead of night and abducted two of the villagers. The next day, U.S. and ARVN soldiers were helpless. They needed a way to trace the guerillas themselves, and also a way to follow them back to their enclave where perhaps a larger force could be eliminated, and so they thought of using tracker dogs.

The only experience Americans had had with trackers dogs was back in 1830, when bloodhounds were used to track Indians in the Second Seminole War. Fortunately, Americans were aware that during World War II Britain had initiated a very successful tactic called "recce" patrols, for finding pockets of Japanese soldiers hidden on the Pacific Islands. The British trained their tracker dogs at the Jungle Warfare School in Malaysia. In 1966, Britain allowed the U.S. to begin training 14 tracker teams there as well.

The purpose of the tracker team is to find retreating or evading enemy troops, but not to engage with them. Black or yellow Labrador retrievers were preferred, because of their strong ability to scent on the ground. In contrast to scout dogs, which will alert to any unfamiliar odor, a tracker dog is trained specifically to follow only one scent on the ground. The dog learns the scent by sniffing a footprint or blood spot, which provides the dog with a unique, signature smell that he can discern among the hundreds already on the path.

A Yellow Labrador Retreiver

During their months of training, tracker dogs are not taught to attack, or to alert to booby traps or trip wires, although of course many do.

In 1968, the U.S. Army started training its own tracker dogs at Fort Gordon, Georgia. That same year, they sent ten tracker teams to Vietnam and added another ten teams in 1969. These were scattered throughout South Vietnam, often in the same locations as scout dog platoons.

The only flaw in this strategy was that tracker teams were sometimes ambushed, because dogs trained to follow a ground scent weren't trained to alert when the enemy was near. Some tracker teams began to work with scout dog teams, but this didn't happen routinely. Unfortunately, there was no coordination within the military so that the dogs' skills could be used most effectively.

DIET AND DISEASE TAKE THEIR TOLL

Most dogs who served in Vietnam didn't die from enemy fire – in fact, only ten percent were wounded or killed in action. Most of the rest of the dogs who died during the war were victims of poor diet and diseases indigenous to Indochina.

To begin with, the dog food provided to handlers for their dogs was of poor quality. Despite a Veterinary Corps report in 1959 recommending an improvement, the food's nutritional value was very low. Domestic pet dogs back in the United States ate better than their hardworking counterparts in Vietnam. Anzo, a German shepherd assigned to John Keith in 1967, ate four pounds of dog food a day at the base camp kennel, and two pounds a day out in the field. Despite this prodigious appetite, the dog, who had weighed 80 pounds on his arrival in

Vietnam, weighed only 67 pounds a year later when he was killed by a booby trap. The cereal-based diet dogs were given in Vietnam also caused many of them bloating and gastro-intestinal problems.

In 1966, thousands of pounds of dog food were found to be rancid, moldy, and full of insects and weevils. It took the deaths of eight sentry dogs for the army to attempt to improve the situation.

Their solution was to mix a commercial brand of dry dog food with horsemeat, and pack it into five-gallon containers. Although this was an improvement, an increasing shortage of horsemeat made it difficult to continue manufacturing the improved food.

The Air Force developed what was purported to be the best food possible nutritionally available for dogs during Vietnam, but it wasn't shipped overseas until 1971, when the drawdown of military forces there was in full swing. It had plenty of calories and included disease preventatives for heartworm and hookworm. But it was high in fat and low in fiber, which created loose stools and extra work for handlers to keep the kennels clean.

The dog food also didn't taste good to dogs, and getting them to eat it instead of the soldiers' rations was a constant challenge.

WINSTON, THE HUNGRY SENTRY

Craig Lord was 20 years old in January, 1969, when he was stationed at Phan Rang Air Base as a sentry dog handler. His dog's name was Winston, and their job was to secure the vulnerable air base from attacks.

When Lord and Winston went out on duty, they first picked up their C-rations (food rations). It seemed like one of the biggest battles they had to fight – who would get what C-rations. Beans and Weenies were one of Lord's favorites, because they had less grease than the soldiers' normal rations; there were also real beans and hotdogs, and some crackers and chocolate for dessert. Everyone liked Beans and Weenies, so there was never enough for everyone. Sometimes Lord waited for some days, only to be stuck with the lima beans.

One night, finally, Lord got his hands on some Beans and Weenies. He and Winston were dropped at their duty post, and began their rounds of the air base perimeter. The moon was out, the night was quiet, Lord had his Beans and Weenies, and all was well. When it was time to eat, Lord began heating up his meal on a sterno stove. While it was cooking, he relieved himself in some nearby bushes.

He had left Winston off his leash for just that one moment, and when he returned, it was to see Winston grabbing the can off the stove. The dog pushed his mouth into the can and held his snout up high, eating, with bean juice dripping down his nose. By the time Lord got to him, Winston had eaten all the hotdogs and most of the beans, and left some saliva in the can for good measure. Lord was mad, and worked Winston hard that night. But before long, he had forgiven his dog. He knew that Winston deserved some good food now and then too.

DISEASE

Disease was another problem for the war dogs. In 1967, many dogs began to suffer from a disease called tropical canine pancytopenia (TCP). A dog would get a fever for a few days or weeks, and then appear to recover. But, several months later, he would begin bleeding from the nose, lose his appetite, and develop weak hind legs. Death would come a few days later. By 1969, the disease became so common that some dog platoons lost half their dogs. Eventually, it was discovered that ticks brought by the Malaysian tracker dogs were carrying the disease. Tetracycline treated the problem, but didn't remove it from a sick dog's bloodstream, which meant that it continued to be passed to other dogs.

Chapter Nine

Abandoned:
The End of the
Vietnam War

Best Friends

By 1969, the U.S. had begun to withdraw from Vietnam. Almost everyone who had worked with or near a dog agreed that the war dogs had more than pulled their share of the load. But what was rarely articulated was the fact that dogs were one of the few methods the U.S. military had which allowed them to find the enemy before the enemy found them. The evasive nature of the Vietcong guerrillas was one of the most difficult elements of a confounding war, and dogs, to a small extent, were able to reduce that problem.

Although the number of dog teams in Vietnam wasn't large enough to affect the outcome of the war, it is estimated that the 4,000 dogs there saved as many as 10,000 lives. Missions with dogs suffered fewer casualties than missions without dogs, and had more canines been present, there would have been fewer dead or maimed soldiers. Many handlers credited their dogs with saving their lives.

Dogs also had a big impact on soldiers' mental health. A dog's unwavering devotion and warm physical presence provided great comfort to a soldier suffering from the stress of not knowing whether he would survive the day. Many stories show the depth of the bond which developed between dogs and their handlers.

MISS CRACKER, THE SCOUT DOG

Robert Himrod and his dog, Miss Cracker, were on patrol near Saigon in 1968, when Himrod heard a small noise. He jerked back as quickly as he could on Miss Cracker's leash, but a booby trap exploded. Himrod was able to hit the ground and avoid the blast, but his dog's leash became entangled on a tree limb, and she took the full force of the bomb. Himrod was hit by a piece of shrapnel, and man and dog were both airlifted from the site. In the helicopter, Miss Cracker suddenly stopped breathing. Without hesitation, Himrod put his mouth over hers and tried to give her mouth-to-mouth resuscitation, but she died a short time later. He believed that he owed his life to Miss Cracker, and he would have done anything to try to save hers in return.

MAJOR, THE GERMAN SHEPHERD SAVED BY HIS MASTER

Marine Ralph McWilliams and his dog Major were on a reconnaissance patrol near Da Nang in 1967 when they were attacked by guerillas. Four Vietcong were killed, but Major was wounded in the leg by a small piece of shrapnel. The patrol was still not out of danger, and they began moving toward their helicopter pick-up point and safety. That little piece of shrapnel was big enough to stiffen the dog's leg so it was difficult for him to walk, and he was slowing down the entire patrol. The commanding officer ordered McWilliams to kill Major so they could press ahead. But man and dog had been through a lot together during their three months as a team.

"He had saved my life several times," said McWilliams, "so the least I could do was try to save his." McWilliams lifted the 90-pound tawny German shepherd, and carried him for nearly two miles to the pick-up point. "I just couldn't destroy him like that," said McWilliams. "His wound may have been slowing the patrol's progress, but he wasn't hurt bad enough to destroy him for humane reasons...I figured I owed him a chance to live."

BRUISER, THE SAVIOR OF HIS MASTER

John Flannelly was on a mission in September, 1969, when his dog Bruiser alerted. In a documentary entitled "War Dogs...America's Forgotten Heroes," he tells the following story.

"Bruiser stopped dead, nose up, ears twitching. I noticed some movement in the bush. I chose to fire, and the next thing I know, all hell breaks loose. I looked down and I thought my arm was blown off. My whole side was open. I could watch my left lung filling up and down and then slowly deflate. Bruiser was just standing there, looking down at me with a very sad look in his eyes. He knew we were in way over our heads. And I didn't want him to be there. I didn't want him to have to see me die. I said, 'Bruiser, go!' Every time I spoke I was spitting up blood. I was just trying to stay conscious. But he wouldn't leave. I wanted to get him out of there before I died.

"He reached down and tried to bite into part of my uniform by my shoulder. I grabbed onto the body harness that the dogs wore and he dragged me back. I don't know how far it was. It seemed like forever. I don't know where he got the strength and he was dragging me, and even though he was hit two times, he was determined to get me out of there. His loyalty was immeasurable. I'll never be able to thank him enough for that. I owe my life to that dog."

PAPER, THE HERO DOG WHO SAVED HIS MASTER AND HIS PLATOON

Tom Hewitt, of the 42nd Scout Dog Platoon, is another vet who tells his story in the "War Dogs" documentary. Hewitt's dog Paper had already been critically wounded once. Hewitt carried Paper for three days to get him out of the jungle to a vet, where, despite orders for him to be put down, Paper survived and went back on duty after a ten-week recovery period.

Three days after going back on duty, Hewitt and Paper were hastily ordered out on an emergency mission to rescue a village under enemy attack. When they reached the village, Hewitt tells of the following events:

"Paper moved in within 30 yards of the hooch and he spun around real quick. I'll never forget. It was like, 'They're here,' and you knew he was close to the enemy.

"By the time I turned around and signaled to the platoon, they cut loose on us. Paper and I were in the center of it - caught in the crossfire. I got down and was trying to look up through the grass. I could see him the whole time, crawling on the ground, trying to get back to me. I could see the trails of bullets. They were taking shots at him. I remember when he got back to me how he cuddled up to me. He was laying so close to me, I just couldn't believe it. So I reached back and said, 'Paper,' and as I reached back I could feel half his head was missing. I could feel he'd been shot."

Paper had been hit by a bullet that would have killed Hewitt. And his alert had saved the entire platoon from being cut down by enemy fire. Despite his knowledge that Paper's wound was fatal, Hewitt carried the dog to a Medivac unit.

ANZO, THE DOG HIS HANDLER DIDN'T WANT TO LEAVE BEHIND

John Keith, a handler with the 2nd Marine Scout Dog Platoon, had trained Anzo, a three-year-old German shepherd, at Fort Benning, Georgia, for four intensive months in late 1966. The two ended up first in their class of 45 scout dog teams, as measured by number of enemy kills and ammunition finds during simulated combat.

Forming a friendship hadn't been easy – Anzo bit Keith several times, at first, while he was still phasing out his first handler. By the time the pair arrived in Vietnam in early 1967, they were a team.

"It took a while to get to know and understand each little gesture he would make," Keith said at the time, "but now we understand each other real well."

Over the next 12 months, Anzo and Keith went out on 54 reconnaissance patrols. They were responsible for 13 Vietcong deaths, and detected large groups of enemy forces several times. The team was so well known that Retired General Omar Bradley and his wife visited them on a tour through Vietnam that year. "There is no way of telling how many lives he saved," said Keith.

The friendship between Keith and Anzo was so great that when the soldier learned he wouldn't be allowed to take Anzo back to the U.S. when his tour of duty was up, he was despondent. Dogs served for life in Vietnam and were reassigned to new handlers when the old ones left. "I wanted to take him home with me," Keith said. When he found he couldn't, he re-enlisted for another year. Volunteering to return to war was almost unheard of. Keith went home for a 30-day leave, and then returned to Vietnam, and Anzo.

Meanwhile, Anzo was getting a break at base camp. He didn't go on any patrols during Keith's absence because, without an intensive period of retraining, he wouldn't have functioned as well with a different handler. Keith returned to Vietnam in May, 1968. Several months later, in September, Anzo tripped a booby trap, critically wounding his handler and himself. Marines had to shoot Anzo because he wouldn't allow anyone near Keith, who eventually recovered.

No Repatriation for Most War Dogs

Keith's predicament – not knowing until the 11th hour that his dog would have to stay in Vietnam – was standard. Most handlers weren't told that their dogs would stay behind because it would have been too demoralizing, but sooner or later everyone figured it out.

Despite the experience of World War II, when the U.S. had successfully returned dogs to their owners at home after the war was over, the military decided that dogs who served in Vietnam were not to be repatriated. The reasons for this change in policy were unclear, but it may have been caused in part because civilians were not involved in procuring dogs for this war to the extent they had been in World War II. Many top brass also mistakenly thought that the dogs were too vicious to ever return to domestic life. Whereas World War II dogs received certificates inscribed with "Honorable Discharge," the Vietnam canines were classified as "equipment," and, like tanks and other articles of war, they were left behind as soldiers departed.

This choice was justified as being practical and logical, because shipping dogs home cost money and required substantial planning. But decisions which come from the head and ignore the heart are not always the wisest. The mental toll on dog handlers was huge. Many wanted to take their animals home with them, particularly the scout and tracker dogs, who were not as vicious as sentry dogs. Some soldiers went to great lengths to try to get their dogs sent home with them.

WOLF STAYS BEHIND

When Charlie Cargo's tour of duty was up in 1971 and he was about to be shipped home, he found he couldn't bear to leave Wolf. Earlier in the year, he had deliberately mouthed off to a superior to lose his promotion from the rank of sergeant so that he wouldn't be separated from his dog. But this time, his efforts failed. Back home, his family called senior officers dozens of times, trying to get Wolf shipped home with Cargo. When that didn't work, Cargo tried to get his tour of duty extended so that he could stay with his dog. His request was denied.

On December 7, 1971, with a heavy heart, Cargo took his best friend to the dog detachment center near Saigon. Cargo said it was the worst day of his life.

"I will never forget the confusion on Wolf's face when I walked away forever," he said "it was like someone just ripped out my heart." To make it worse, Cargo was uncertain of Wolf's ultimate fate for 30 years. Only recently did he discover that Wolf was one of the few dogs lucky enough to be returned to the United States. In March, 1972, Wolf was taken to Lackland Air Force Base in Texas and operated on for testicular cancer. He went back to work until he died in 1979. To this day, Cargo still wears a wristband made from Wolf's collar.

Unfortunately, Wolf was one of only several hundred dogs to be returned home after the war. In 1970, the American public learned of the decision to leave the war dogs in Vietnam, and the military scrambled to respond to the uproar. The press wrote articles, and several congressmen attempted to pass bills to save the animals, but they never reached a vote. The military, recognizing the need for damage control, adopted a policy designed to appease the public. They announced that all "healthy" dogs would be allowed to return, knowing full well that most dogs in Vietnam had picked up infectious diseases. In 1971, a plane transported only 120 dogs out of Vietnam.

Of the 4,000 dogs in Vietnam, almost 500 were listed as Killed in Action. Most of the rest of the dogs were turned over to the ARVN, who really didn't want them. One handler, named Tony Montoya, was assigned the job of delivering some dogs to the ARVN on the air base at Bien Hoa. He said that the dogs were bigger than the Vietnamese, who were clearly scared of the canines. They considered the black Labrador trackers bad luck, and wanted no part of them. The handlers knew that the Vietnamese viewed dogs differently than Americans, and many suspected that the ARVN were eating the dogs. One platoon was reported to have put down its dogs rather than leave them to an unknown fate.

The heroes who had saved so many lives were doomed to suffer an igno-
minious end.

CLIPPER STAYS BEHIND

John Burnam's old knee injury was bothering him so much by January,
1967, that it became difficult for him to walk. He was ordered off combat duty, and then moved to a different base away from his scout dog
platoon and his dog Clipper to serve out the remainder of his
tour of duty.

Being removed from combat was fine with Burnam, who believed
that walking point was bound to get him killed sooner or later. But he
missed his fellow dog handlers, and most of all, his dog. Clipper was
well taken care of during Burnam's absence, and he was not reassigned
to another handler until Burnam left Vietnam. But as the months
passed, Burnam missed Clipper's companionship and playfulness.

Burnam wrote, "I longed to have him sit next to me and lean
against my leg when he was tired. I wanted to watch him get excited to
hear me call his name. I missed the simple pleasure of having Clipper
with me all the time. It was tormenting not to be able to see my dog."

Before he flew out of Vietnam for good, Burnam made a last trip to
Dau Tieng to say goodbye to Clipper. Burnam's reunion with his best
friend was joyful, and he couldn't bear to think of parting from the dog
again. They took a walk together, and then Burnam put Clipper
through some basic commands. The next morning, he got up early to
say goodbye.

His sorrow was made more poignant by the knowledge that Clipper
would never leave Vietnam. Clipper had saved Burnam's life countless
times, and many other soldiers' lives had been saved by his early alerts

as well. He was a hero, yet he would never be welcomed home as a hero should be. Burnam couldn't hide the tears when he said his final good-bye to Clipper, and walked away.

RECOGNITION COMES

As America's wounds from the Vietnam war began to heal, some former dog handlers got together to create the Vietnam Dog Handler's Association (VDHA), an organization which is devoted to keeping the memory of war dogs and their actions alive. Although there are many memorials honoring Vietnam veterans, until recently there were very few memorials honoring dogs who served in wars. The Hartsdale Pet Cemetery in New York built the first monument to war dogs in 1918, in honor of those heroes of World War I. Dogs who served with the Marines in World War II are honored by statues in Guam and at the University of Tennessee. But not until 2000 were there memorials for the Vietnam war dogs. Although the VDHA had talked about creating a memorial for years, they didn't have funding.

Help came when Jeffrey Bennett, president and CEO of Nature's Recipe Pet Foods, agreed to produce a documentary called "War Dogs: America's Forgotten Heroes," which aired on public television stations in 1999, and is still being shown. The documentary is filled with emotional interviews with former dog handlers, and reenactments of actual battles. The film raised awareness, and contributions to the memorial increased. In 2000, two memorials were dedicated specifically to the war dogs who served in Vietnam. One is at March Field Air Museum in Riverside, California, and a second was erected at Fort Benning, Georgia, the site where many dogs received their training. Now the VDHA is spearheading a drive to erect a national memorial.

Meanwhile, another group of concerned war dog advocates began lobbying to end the military policy of killing dogs who could no longer work. This drew public and presidential attention. In November 2000, President Bill Clinton signed into law HR 5314. This law specified that the Department of Defense release old and infirm war dogs to their handlers, civilian law enforcement agencies, or other responsible civilians.

Maybe now U.S. dog heroes will begin to get the respect and homecoming they deserve. And perhaps human beings are starting to acknowledge the debts they owe to animals. War dogs should be treated as respectfully as war veterans should be, and allowed to end their days in the peaceful homes they have fought for.

Note: Page numbers in *italics* refer to
    captions to illustrations

Books

Behan, John M. *Dogs of War*,(Charles Scribner's Sons, New York, 1946)

Burnam, John C. *Dog Tags of Courage: The Turmoil of War and the Rewards of Companionship*, (Lost Coast Press, Fort Bragg, CA, 2000)

Downey, Fairfax. *Dogs for Defense*, (McDonald, New York, 1955)

Going, Clayton G. *Dogs at War*, (The MacMillan Company, New York, 1944)

Grow, Malcolm C. *Surgeon Grow: An American in the Russian Fighting*, (Frederick A. Stokes, 1918)

Lemish, Michael G. *War Dogs: A History of Loyalty and Heroism*, (Brassey's, Washington, D.C 1996)

Lubow, Robert E. *The War Animals*, (Doubleday and Co., New York, 1977)

Morgan, Paul B. *K-9 Soldiers: Vietnam and After* (Hellgate Press, Central Point, OR 1999)

Rohan, Jack. *Rags: The Story of a Dog who Went to War*, (Harper, New York, 1930)

Ross, Estelle, *The Book of Noble Dogs*, (Century Co., New York, 1922)

Sanderson, Jeannette. *War Dog Heroes: True Stories of Dog Courage in Wartime*, (Scholastic Inc., New York, 1997)

Seguin, Marilyn W. *Dogs of War and Stories of Other Beasts of Battle in the Civil War*, (Branden Publishing Company, Brookline Village, MA, 1998)

Terhune, Albert Payson. *A Book of Famous Dogs*, (Doubleday, Doran and Company, Inc., Garden City, N.Y 1937)

Thurston, Elizabeth. *The Lost History of the Canine Race: Our 15,000-year Love Affair with Dogs*, (Avon, 1997)

Web sites

http://community-2.webtv.net/Hahn-50thAP-K9/K9History11
http://www.qmfound.com/War_Dogs.htm
http://www.scoutdogpages.com/wolfcharlie.htm
http://www.vdhaonline.org./arch_9th.html
http://www.geocities.com/Pentagon/4759
http://www.fortunecity.com/skyscraper/backspace/1818/forgotten3.htm
http://www.vietnamwar.net/robert/robert.htm
http://www.antiquesatoz.com/stephenherold.vc.vclist06.htm
http://www.stemnet.nf.ca/CITE/newfoundland_gander_hero.htm
http://www.miniatures.de/html/int/shellsRu/html
http://www.netcomuk.c.uk/~dpohara/mouse.htm

Documentary

Wars Dogs: America's Forgotten Heroes (GRB Entertainment)

The publishers would like to thank the following sources for their kind permission
to reproduce the pictures in this book:

John Daniels: 1, 18, 23, 28, 34, 36, 58, 62, 70, 82, 100, 123, 132, 140

RSPCA Photolibrary: David Dalton 11; Cheryl E Ertelt, 86, 88, 113; EA Janes,
20, 74; Colin Sedon 46

Every effort has been made to acknowledge correctly and contact the source and/or copyright
holder of each picture, and Carlton Books Limited apologises for any unintentional errors or
ommissions which will be corrected in future editions of this book.